THE VIKING DIG

York Archaeological Trust's excavation in Coppergate
between 1976 and 1981 revealed what life in the city
was like between the departure of the Roman Legion
c.400 AD, and the arrival of the Normans in 1068.

Waterlogged soil had preserved the remains of
tenth-century houses and workshops, and a range of
everyday items unparalleled anywhere in England,
including leather shoes, textiles and wooden objects.
Evidence for crafts and industry painted a vivid picture
of York's thriving mercantile economy. Microscopic
environmental data—seeds, pollen, insect remains,
animal, fish and bird bones—allowed living conditions
to be reconstructed. This book describes not only these
Viking Age discoveries, but also the other notable finds
of the Roman town, a superb Anglo-Saxon helmet,
medieval buildings and associated objects.

The Excavations at York

THE VIKING DIG

Richard Hall

THE BODLEY HEAD
LONDON

To Linda

British Library Cataloguing
In Publication Data
Hall, Richard
The Viking Dig
The Excavations at York
1. Northern-England
2. York (North Yorkshire)—
Antiquities
1. Title
936.2′843 DA690.Y6
ISBN 0–370–30802–6 (hardback)
0–370–30821–2 (paperback)
© Richard Hall 1984
Printed in Great Britain for
The Bodley Head Ltd
30 Bedford Square, London, WC1B 3RP by
William Clowes Ltd, Beccles
Set by Wyvern Typesetting Ltd, Bristol
First published 1984
Reprinted 1986

Contents

Acknowledgements

The spectacular discoveries made during the Coppergate excavation were the direct result of York City Council's far-sighted decision to facilitate archaeological investigation on this site well in advance of proposed redevelopment. If such a dovetailing of archaeology and redevelopment became standard practice much more of Britain's buried heritage could be saved from needless destruction. In the final stages of the excavation the site's development contractors, Wimpey Property Holdings Ltd and their constructional firm Wimpey Construction Ltd, were also extremely sympathetic to archaeological requirements, and continued this policy throughout the archaeological watching brief which accompanied construction work.

The excavation was funded in part from the rescue archaeology budget of the Inspectorate of Ancient Monuments at the Department of the Environment, where successive Inspectors and their superiors responded sympathetically to the project's requirements. Additional funds were donated privately by interested individuals, trust funds and companies: I hope that other benefactors will not take it amiss if the substantial help given by The British Academy, the Tjaereborg Foundation, Rowntree Macintosh Ltd and C. I. Skipper Esq is singled out for mention here. An attempt at a complete roll of donors is found on pp. 154–5 although even here oversights may have occurred and will, I hope, be forgiven.

Within York Archaeological Trust thanks are due primarily to the permanent excavation team who worked hard and skilfully while enduring rain and snow, flood and frost (as well as the heatwave summer of 1976). Among them Sue Winterbottom, Jeff Peters, Liz Neville, Margaret Nieke, Sue Duffy, Julian Richards, Nick Price, Lawrence Manley and Dave Start made particularly notable contributions over long periods. The Area Supervisors had a particularly heavy responsibility on a complex site and with a variable workforce; they included David Evans (1976–81), Shahed Power (1976–8), Mick Humphreys (1976–8) and Ian Lawton (1978–81). Nick Pearson took charge of the watching brief in 1981–2.

Behind the archaeological front line was ranged the expertise and dedication of all the Trust's staff, for example in fund-raising, conservation and administration, and their considerable contribution to the excavation must not be overlooked. The photographs reproduced here are the work of Mike Duffy, except for Plates 5–9 (author), 149–51 (John Bailey) and 177 (Ryszard Bartkowiak). The illustrations of objects are by Sheena Howarth, except for Fig. 102 (Ailsa Mainman) and Figs 21, 31–2, 53, 58, 104, 112, 115, 119, 121b, 129, 131, 138 and 140 which are by Helen Humphreys, who also drew the plans and diagrams. I am particularly grateful to Arthur MacGregor and Dominic Tweddle, successively in charge of research on the excavated objects, for their expert advice, and this debt extends to the many specialists from all over Britain and beyond who have commented on particular aspects of the excavated material. Among them Harry Kenward, Allan Hall, Terry O'Connor and Andrew Jones, Research Fellows of the Environmental Archaeology Unit at York University, and Enid Allison, a post-graduate research student there; Justine Bayley of the Department of the Environment's Archaeological Research Laboratory (metal and glass-working residues); Penny Walton (textiles); Ruth Jones and Jennifer Hillam of Sheffield University's dendrochronology laboratory; Ailsa Mainman and Catherine Brooks (Viking Age and medieval pottery); Jean Dawes (human skeletal material); and Elizabeth Pirie (Leeds City Museum), Christopher Blunt and the late Michael Dolley (numismatica), have probably answered the greatest number of questions. I hope I have represented their opinions accurately in what follows, and take full responsibility for any errors there may be.

Finally, I should like to acknowledge the contribution of the members of the Trust, their Executive Committee and Officers, and to thank the Trust's Director, P. V. Addyman, for his support throughout.

R.A.H.

Foreword by
HRH The Prince of Wales

In 1976 York Archaeological Trust began excavating at Coppergate, attracted by the reputation of this part of York for throwing up Viking finds whenever development disturbed the ground. As so often happens nowadays it was a rescue dig, in which archaeologists strive to salvage the buried past before bulldozers sweep it away for ever. The expected Viking remains proved to be there at Coppergate, superbly preserved in the waterlogged ground, but there was far more. The site contained a complete slice of York's history from Roman times to the present. The struggle to record these remains before a new shopping centre destroyed them became itself something of a saga worthy of the Vikings.

As a patron of the excavation I was able to watch the saga unfold. Like half a million others I visited the site at Coppergate. I was able to follow progress in the Trust's bulletins from the workfront and I appreciated only too well the need for funds and resources. I saw some of the results of the dig in the international exhibition *The Vikings in England*. I have also met many of the people from various parts of the world who have generously supported the Trust in its efforts to preserve this part of our past, and I share the satisfaction that future generations will be able to see the results of our work in the underground Jorvik Viking Centre, built on the dig site itself at Coppergate.

In this book Richard Hall, the director of the dig, leads us through this saga. It is a complicated story. With him we are able to visit this much inhabited half acre of land time and time again—in the Roman, Anglian, Viking, Norman and medieval ages. We learn something of the problems encountered by modern archaeologists and the methods they use to recover a story like this. I commend this book for several reasons. It provides a record of one of the great excavations of the 1970s and it gives us insights into the historical importance of York in various periods of the nation's past. Most important of all, it highlights the challenge which faces our generation to save at least some part of the past for the future. The story of Coppergate may, I hope, provide an inspiration for others to take similar opportunities, not only in York but in other historic cities in Britain.

Charles

Introduction

Between May 1976 and September 1981 over half a million people paid an entrance fee to visit a demolition site at 16–22 Coppergate in York. What compelled them to stare at a large, deep and often muddy hole in the ground? Why did the site receive national and international attention from radio, television and the press, with articles appearing in such far-flung newspapers as *Sydsvenska Dagbladet* and *The Minneapolis Daily*? Above all, why did HM Queen Margrethe of Denmark, HRH the Prince of Wales, HRH Crown Prince Harald of Norway and HE the President of Iceland come to see the site for themselves?

This large hole in the centre of York was 'The Viking Dig', an archaeological excavation by York Archaeological Trust which gave the city's inhabitants and the visitor alike a first opportunity to glimpse the buried remains of Viking Age York. For many people the excavation became an absorbing race against time to learn as much as possible before redevelopment began. This race turned out to be a marathon, for thanks to a series of postponements and delays in the planning of the redevelopment York Archaeological Trust was eventually allowed over five years of uninterrupted excavation.

This book summarises and illustrates the main discoveries not only from the Viking Age but also from the Roman, Anglo-Saxon and medieval layers on the site. It would be impossible to unfold the discoveries in the day-to-day sequence in which they were made without creating a rather patchy and episodic story, for circumstances dictated that remains of different periods were often being excavated simultaneously on different parts of the site. Instead, the whole picture for each main period will be described, starting with the earliest remains and working towards the present day to show how the site gradually developed. A summary of York's history and an outline of previous archaeological discoveries there are provided first, in order to set the Coppergate excavation in a wider perspective.

Throughout the text, illustrations are referred to by numbers enclosed within brackets; numbers in bold type are those of coloured plates. The frontispiece illustrates the Viking Dig in progress in 1981, and the interlace animal decoration on page 1 is on the nasal from the Coppergate Anglo-Saxon helmet. The coin on the front of the jacket is a raven penny of Olaf Guthfrithsson, King of York 939–41.

1
Background to an Excavation

The story of York over the last two thousand years is one of a series of continental invaders—Romans, Anglo-Saxons, Vikings and Normans—who successively realised the site's advantages and made the city their home. Founded as a Roman military base c. AD 71, and augmented by the gradual growth of a substantial Roman civilian town, York's excellent defensive position and its good natural communications by land and water ensured that future immigrants would find it equally attractive (2). For the Anglo-Saxon kings of Northumbria in the seventh, eighth and early ninth centuries it became a royal site, a centre for the church with its archbishopric and monastic school, and also an important international trading centre and distribution point. The Vikings captured it in 866, enlarged it, and made it the capital of their only lasting independent kingdom in England—the Viking kingdom of York. This kingdom, corresponding approximately to the county of Yorkshire, was ruled by Danish and Norwegian kings until 954 and then incorporated into the newly forged kingdom of England, but there was a strong Scandinavian element in the population up to the Norman period and beyond. When William the Conqueror took control in 1068 York was the second largest and richest city in England, and it was to remain the 'capital of the north' throughout the medieval centuries. Subsequently, while the city continued to be a social centre, the Industrial Revolution and

Victorian rebuilding largely passed it by, and so York reached the twentieth century with a remarkable legacy of visible remains dating back to its earliest days, and a wealth of largely undisturbed buried archaeological remains unsurpassed for range and variety in any other British city.

The pace of redevelopment in York quickened in the 1950s and gradually it was realised that new buildings in the ancient city centre were destroying large amounts of the buried evidence for York's earlier history. The largest single threat came in 1972 with plans for an inner ring road, which was carefully routed to involve the minimum disturbance to buildings of historical and architectural significance, but which would have destroyed parts of several Roman cemeteries and cut swathes across the city's medieval suburbs, including in all eighteen known archaeological sites.

The response to this potential archaeological blight was the establishment of York Archaeological Trust, an independent charity directed by Peter Addyman, with a staff of full-time professional archaeologists including both excavators and a back-up team of photographers, draughtsmen, conservators and researchers. The funding for this came largely from the Department of the Environment's Ancient Monuments Inspectorate, with other contributions from site developers, various academic and charitable trusts and local authorities. The Trust's brief was to investigate sites within

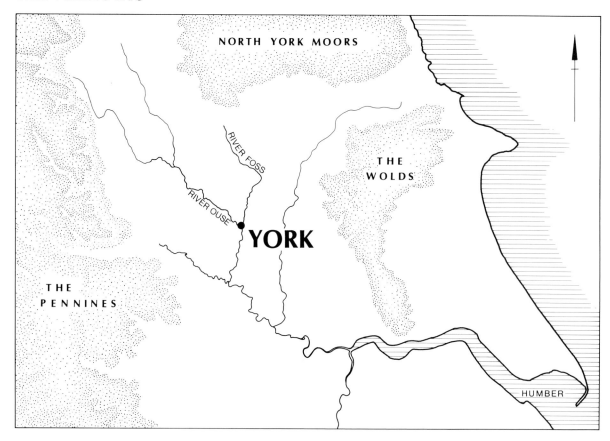

2 York's geographical setting.

York which were to be destroyed in redevelopments, and although the ring-road scheme was eventually abandoned the Trust has been busy ever since, excavating on sites of all periods, whenever they are threatened.

One of the first excavations the Trust undertook in 1972 became necessary when Lloyds Bank decided to extend their premises at the corner of Pavement and Piccadilly (4), and to construct new vaults below. This is precisely the part of York which had yielded up the largest group of typically Viking Age jewellery, weapons, tools and domestic items, found by chance during earlier building works. Although these objects were not carefully excavated from well-dated layers, and could not tell a coherent story of life in the Viking Age city of Jorvik, they did show that archaeological remains could be identified which corresponded to the historical records of Vikings living in the city, and suggested that this was an important commercial area in the Viking Age town.

During the winter of 1972–3 a small Trust team worked in the basement of 6–8 Pavement, excavating four shafts each two metres square. Archaeological deposits—that is, layers representing human activity, occupation or desertion of the site, rather than a purely natural accumulation—extended down to over nine metres below the present street level, and included a substantial block of Viking Age layers of ninth- and tenth-century date. Such a build-up of buried remains is exceptional in England, and consists of layer after layer of building remains and domestic rubbish, with one intermediate band of sterile soil representing a period when the site was deserted and left to the elements. The proximity of the River Foss kept all the layers damp, and this moist soil allowed the preservation of timber building remains and fragile objects made from organic materials—wood, textile, leather— which rot to dust on the normal, dry archaeological site. Their preservation gave a much more complete picture of life in the Viking Age than would normally be possible—for example, not only did we find iron knife blades, but also wooden handles for the knives, and the decorated leather sheaths into which they fitted. In fact, so many leather scraps were found, as well as boots and shoes and two shoemaker's wooden lasts, that we suspected that the timber buildings were probably occupied by shoemakers and cobblers in the Viking Age.

More light was shed upon the living conditions of the leatherworkers through another form of evidence whose value had at that time been recognised by only a few people. This was an integrated study of insect, plant and soil remains to build up a picture of the ancient environment. These remains, many of which are microscopic, are also well preserved in moist soil, and their study at the Lloyds Bank site presented many new details of life in Anglo-Scandinavian York. For example, rotting plant and animal matter had been common-place and the areas outside the buildings had been rather moist and foul, but indoors conditions may not have been too unpleasant. There was evidence that meat, fish, shellfish and birds were eaten, as well as cereals, fruits and nuts. Hunger was intensified by the human intestinal parasites which betrayed their presence through their microscopic eggs. If not all human life, then at least much of it seemed to be represented in the environmental data.

The Lloyds Bank excavation allowed the first detailed examination of York's Viking Age or Anglo-Scandinavian archaeology, and showed that an exceptional richness of archaeological informa-tion awaited discovery in the deeply stratified moist soils. But Jorvik had been a city of almost two thousand dwellings in 1066, according to Domesday Book, and Lloyds Bank provided a key-hole glimpse

of only two. What did complete houses and workshops of the ninth and tenth centuries look like? What other crafts and industries were carried on? What did the people wear? How did they spend their time? The basic questions still had no answer, and there was only one way to find out—to excavate on a much larger scale on a site near by where the same favourable conditions could be expected.

The opportunity presented itself quite soon, when York City Council redirected their attention to two adjacent derelict properties which they had acquired in 1966 and 1970, the White Horse public house and Craven's sweet factory in Coppergate, just seventy metres from the Lloyds Bank site (4). The Council's initial idea was to redevelop this site, and to follow this with further redevelopment at an adjacent car park in Piccadilly, by the River Foss, and then at another adjacent car park at Castlegate, around the Norman and later castle. However, the gloomy economic outlook meant that 1975 was not a time when developers were likely to be interested in a scheme of this size and expense, and so it seemed probable that the Coppergate buildings would continue to stand empty for some time. For York Archaeological Trust this represented a chance to undertake large-scale work in a key area without delaying an eager developer, and so the Department of the Environment was approached to see if finance would be available, and the City Council was asked if demolition of the derelict buildings could be brought forward to allow excavation to start. Money was promised, and after an initial refusal the Council changed its mind and demolition work began.

Meanwhile, the Trust began to marshal its resources—excavations take a lot of careful plan-ning. Fortunately, the nucleus of an excavation team which had only just finished work at another site in York was available for transfer to Coppergate. It included two Area Supervisors, whose job would be to supervise excavation and recording within their specified parts of the site, and about a dozen experienced excavation assistants, employed on a semi-permanent basis. This team would be rein-forced during the summer months and at Easter by 'experienced volunteers'—normally young people,

usually students (not necessarily of archaeology), who enjoy working on excavations in their vacations, and who already know the basic techniques. They are not purely volunteers in the financial sense, as they require accommodation and a subsistence payment, but they are a useful pool of temporary additional labour, particularly in the summer when the weather should allow work to proceed faster than at other times. So they too were recruited, both from Britain and beyond—during the excavation up to forty per cent of the volunteers were from abroad, coming from Denmark, Norway, Sweden, the USA, Canada, France, Germany, Spain, Holland, Switzerland, Poland and Hungary.

The Trust also continued its practice of having a small group of workers from among the residents of Thorp Arch open prison. At our expense, up to four

3 HRH The Prince of Wales at Coppergate with the author and York Archaeological Trust's Director, Peter Addyman.

men were transported to and from the site every day, and did much useful work in return for a small tobacco ration. Later, and not simultaneously, a group of women from HM Prison at Askam Grange were also involved in the project on a similar basis until the rising cost of transport made it uneconomic to continue.

From February 1977 onwards another important source of excavating staff was to be the various schemes sponsored by the Trust but paid for by the Manpower Services Commission in its attempt to create jobs for young people. Although totally inexperienced to start with, many of the participants went on to acquire a reasonable degree of proficiency in archaeological methods, and it is certainly true that without them only a fraction of the final result would have been accomplished.

The final group of people who worked at the site were the local part-time amateur archaeologists, the York Excavation Group. Using the same recording methods and techniques as the Archaeological Trust, they excavated their own area at one side of the site, working at weekends and in evenings when light permitted, and their discoveries are incorporated here.

Demolition of the derelict buildings was com-

pleted in May 1976 and immediately the archaeological team began work—not with trowels and hand shovels, but with heavy breakers (pneumatic drills) and sledge-hammers, clearing away the brick and concrete foundations of a suite of modern cellars. This area was chosen as a promising part of the site to start excavation because it was thought that the cellars would have destroyed much of the later medieval layers and so provide us with a short cut into the Viking Age layers. Also, being near Coppergate, which was thought to be a Viking Age street, there was a better chance of finding building remains here than elsewhere. This preliminary clearance took three weeks, the diggers sweltering in

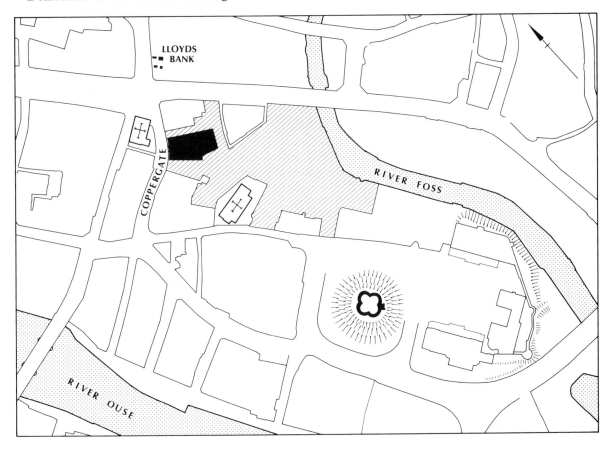

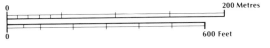

4 The modern plan of the Coppergate area, with the redevelopment site hatched and the excavated area within it.

the blazing sun of one of the hottest summers anyone could recall, and eventually left us with an area bounded towards Coppergate and at both sides by the front and side walls of two cellars, and at the back by a metre-thick concrete raft, a relic of Craven's sweet factory. As the raft was reinforced with three layers of metal rods, we did not relish tackling it at a time when the quality of archaeological remains was still an unknown quantity. It was not possible at that stage to excavate right up to the line of the modern pavement because of the safety requirement to support the pavement and roadway with a solid block of soil—without this buttress, the front of the site, and with it pedestrians and traffic, would all have been in danger of suddenly falling the three metres into the excavated cellar base. Later it was possible to extend forwards to the street frontage and the reinforced cellar base was removed, but the sides of the cellar proved to be convenient limits for excavation throughout the entire project, the space on one side being used as an access route for the heavy machinery needed on site from time to time as well as for a public information centre, and the other side forming a convenient viewing platform for visitors. Thus it was not any sort of intuition which determined the limits of the excavation, but pragmatic reasons.

With summer volunteers it was possible to extend this exploratory phase of work in July 1976 to take in an area further away from Coppergate down one side of the reinforced concrete raft. When modern debris had been removed here, remains of fifteenth/sixteenth century buildings were exposed, at the same absolute level as the Viking Age layers below the cellars near the street frontage. The reason for this apparent anomaly was simply that the site lay over the river terrace of the River Foss, a naturally steep slope which had been gradually levelled since the Roman period.

Within a few months it became obvious that the site was exceeding our highest hopes of the quantity and quality of information we could obtain. But at the same time, at least at the front of the site below the cellars, we were already approaching the limit to which we could dig in safety without somehow

shoring up the edges. Throughout the winter of 1976–7, in what was to become an annual ritual, we hired a covering made from scaffold tubing and polythene sheeting so that we could continue excavating day in and day out without suffering too much from wind, rain, snow and ice (5). This first winter we erected it over the area of later medieval remains where because of modern changes in level across the site we had not yet reached a great depth, and it was therefore safer to continue. The Viking Age levels were covered over as thoroughly as possible and abandoned for the winter.

Although it was hoped that a large part of the project's cost would be covered by Department of the Environment grants over a number of years, this early work made it clear that the scale of the enterprise would require additional funding, particularly for the shoring operation and also for the conservation of the large quantities of fragile organic objects and building remains which we anticipated finding. The likely 'shopping list' of materials and services was a long one, and potential benefactors not obvious. The only possible solution seemed to be the promotion of a fund-raising campaign, and after much debate the local company Borodin Communications Ltd was engaged to undertake a feasibility study. On the basis of this they were then asked to carry out a two-year programme. A strategy of opening the excavation to the public on a grander scale than hitherto, of keeping the media informed of our discoveries, of following up all likely lines of interest, and of sponsoring occasional fund-raising events such as a celebrity book auction, gala theatre performances and social occasions understandably took a long time to recoup the outlay involved, but eventually began to have a significant effect on the level of help offered by industry, individuals, and charitable and academic trusts both throughout Britain and, increasingly, in Scandinavia. A Special Development Programme was initiated to foster the growing interest, and the Trust was honoured when HM Queen Margrethe of Denmark, HM King Carl Gustav of Sweden, HRH the Prince of Wales, HRH Crown Prince Harald of Norway, and HE the President of Iceland all agreed to become Patrons of

the project. A committee of Stewards was also established under the enthusiastic chairmanship of television personality and archaeological writer Magnus Magnusson, incorporating eminent parliamentarians, businessmen and academics who were keen to see the excavation succeed, and it was through their combined efforts and interest that the first major hurdle was cleared, and the finance for shoring the sides of the excavation was assured by a loan on generous terms from the Scandinavian Bank in 1978. This was a particularly expensive operation because the site was surrounded by several delicate medieval buildings which could not withstand the vibrations caused by normal pile-driving. Instead, a hydraulic system which was both noise- and vibration-free had to be employed, at about double the normal cost. Nonetheless, it proved a sound archaeological investment.

Having learned many of the techniques necessary, in 1979 the Trust itself took over the responsibility for the Special Development Programme and with the expertise and acumen of one of its Stewards, Mr Ian Skipper, set up a company called

Cultural Resource Management Ltd to manage and expand the enterprising commercial, resource-gathering and information-giving work already started. With a full-time Manager, Sales Manager, Information Officer and secretary, and controlled ultimately by the Trust to ensure the integrity of the operation,★ CRM's sole purpose was to generate resources to assist the Trust in its archaeological work. To this end an enlarged exhibition was mounted on the Coppergate site, with an audio-visual report on the excavation, explanatory pictures and diagrams, information leaflets, and a shop selling replicas, guide books and souvenirs. Pre-recorded commentaries describing the project were freely available at two points overlooking the site

★ For example, no Vikings wearing horned helmets should adorn the products. Although such helmets are popularly supposed to be an essential piece of Viking equipment, there is no evidence whatsoever that they were ever worn by Viking warriors.

(their day-long operation sometimes driving the diggers nearly to distraction), and large-scale plans keyed to numbered positions in the dig helped the visitors to appreciate what there was to see. Visits by local, national and international pressmen, broadcasters and TV reporters became commonplace. The media interest brought wry comments from most of the diggers, who overheard that the question 'How important is it?' occurred in most interviews; disenchanted with the answers 'very important'/'most important'/'unique', the answer normally murmured from the trenches was a modest 'intergalactic'.

These efforts brought tens of thousands of visitors to the site (6), and generated much goodwill and interest which was also translated into donations of services, equipment and cash. There was never sufficient funding to provide everything that was required, but enough money was raised to allow the team to remain at work continuously until late September 1981, when work on the redevelopment finally began, taking in the excavation site in Coppergate and the adjoining car park in Piccadilly; the car park in Castlegate was left for a future redevelopment. By that time approximately 85 per cent of the archaeological remains at Coppergate had been excavated, including all the medieval, most of the Viking Age and Anglo-Saxon, and over half of the Roman.

The discoveries from all periods were significant and, from the Anglo-Saxon and Anglo-Scandinavian periods, sensational, but they resulted from routine hard work, often undertaken in extremely uncomfortable conditions (7). The working day started at 8.00 am throughout the year, and finished at 4.30 pm; during winter it was generally a five-day week, but in summer six-day weeks were the rule and seven-day weeks not unknown. Nevertheless, the rate of progress sometimes seemed painfully slow, as great care was taken at all stages to recover the maximum possible amount of information; careful excavation was followed by detailed planning, photography and recording before the next layers could be stripped away (8). In all, approximately thirty-four thousand layers were excavated and recorded, each one of them a piece in the vast three-dimensional jigsaw puzzle to be put together by the team writing up the final results of the work.

The excavated objects were dealt with in one of two ways, depending upon which broad category they belonged to. 'Bulk finds'—the common discoveries including pottery, oyster shells, animal bones and tiles—were washed, individually marked in ink with the number of the layer they were found in, and then put into bags and boxes for storage until a specialist was ready to study them. They required the full-time attention of a small team doing nothing else, for they were extremely numerous—for example, it is estimated that the site produced about 230,000 pieces of pottery and five tons of animal bones. Nothing was discarded except the oyster shells which, once they had been counted from each layer, were given away as souvenirs, as they could provide no further information.

The other class of objects was the so-called 'small finds', which could actually be quite large objects; these included all items of obvious individual interest, and others which, while appearing of no great importance, required treatment in the Trust's conservation laboratory (9). More than fifteen thousand 'small finds' were eventually discovered, and each had to be meticulously logged and prepared for storage in an appropriate manner, again a full-time job for at least one person and requiring two or more people at busy times. So as well as the excavation team out on the site, there was a group of finds personnel constantly at work behind the scenes in a basement store retained from demolition at our request, and a back-up team of administrators, photographers, research specialists and outside experts who all contributed to the progress of the work. The results of their endeavours are now to be chronicled.

2
Roman Foundations

The natural soil below the archaeological deposits was easy to recognise—a predominantly yellow silty-sandy clay, which had been laid down either by a glacier melting towards the end of the Ice Age or by river silting since then. The earliest archaeological remains, resting on or cut into this clay, belong to the Roman period, and in this respect Coppergate mirrors every other site excavated in York. Although there may be a small Iron Age farm or farms somewhere under the modern city, and perhaps buildings of even earlier prehistoric date, none has ever been found. The only pre-Roman finds from the area are stone and bronze tools which do not necessarily imply prehistoric occupation, for they may have been abandoned, lost or deliberately buried by prehistoric travellers.

The earliest Roman occupation of York and Yorkshire came c. AD 71, when the IX Legion advanced from an earlier fortress at Lincoln to subdue the Brigantes, the Iron Age tribe occupying much of northern England. The spit of land at the confluence of the rivers Ouse and Foss at York was chosen as the new site for their fortress, called Eburacum, which was first defended by a ditch with an earth bank beyond and timber palisade, watch-towers and gateways. The interior was largely taken up by barrack blocks, with the headquarters building at the centre, the commandant's and officers' houses, a hospital and other standard military buildings, all initially built of timber. Later both the defences and the internal buildings were replaced in stone. Around the fortress other settlements quickly sprang up to cater for the soldiers' off-duty hours. Facing the fortress on the opposite bank of the River Ouse another civilian settlement gradually developed into one of the principal towns of Roman Britain, enclosed by its own wall. Not later than AD 213 it became the capital of Britannia Inferior, one of the two provinces into which Britain was divided. The Emperor Severus, his wife and two sons were resident in York for three years 208–11 while campaigning in Scotland, and the consequent prestige may have brought to York the legal status of *colonia* early in the third century, one of only four towns in Britain to achieve this rank. The Emperor Constantius also visited York and died there in 306—his son Constantine was proclaimed Emperor in the city. By this time York is known to have been an international trading centre and to have contained town houses of some pretension. Yet despite its being the headquarters of northern British military command and a provincial capital, very little is known about Roman York.

In the Roman period the Coppergate area lay outside the walls of the legionary fortress (10). Here should be found the modest structures hastily erected by the various entrepreneurs and camp-followers who accompanied the legion to York in AD 71. They won a living by supplying the needs and pandering to the desires of the legion's six thousand

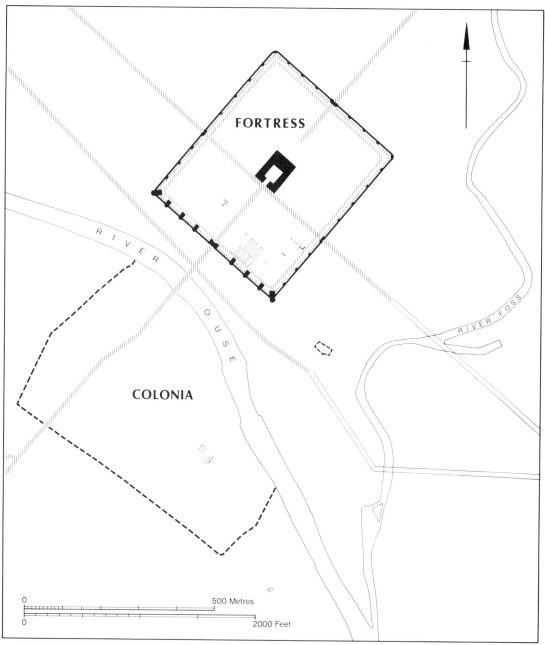

FORTRESS

COLONIA

0
500 Metres
0
2000 Feet

ABOVE
10 Simplified plan of Roman York, showing the location of the Coppergate excavation.

OPPOSITE
6 Crowds viewing the excavation in 1981, with the exhibition facilities behind.

7 Excavating the foundations of Craven's sweet factory.

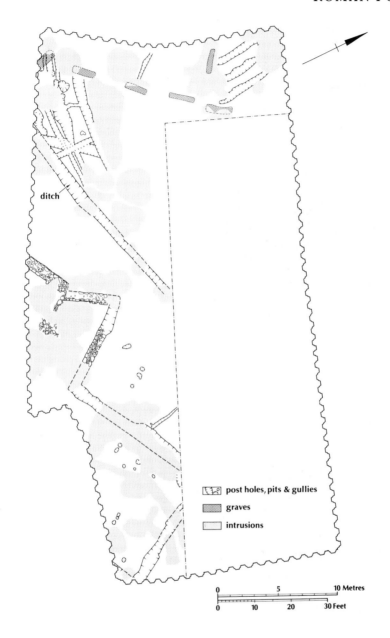

ditch

post holes, pits & gullies

graves

intrusions

0   5   10 Metres

0   10   20   30 Feet

OPPOSITE

8 Drawing the wall of a Viking Age building.

9 Conservation laboratory staff removing a tenth-century timber building for preservation.

ABOVE

11 The Coppergate site during the Roman period, *c.* AD 71–400. Stippling indicates where Roman levels were destroyed by later cuts: the featureless area between the dashed line and the shoring in the north-east part of the site was not investigated at this depth.

17

officers and men. The legion might soon move on, and initially there would be no point in building expensive structures which might be made redundant overnight, but if it seemed that a fortress was a semi-permanent fixture, then the suburbs too might become more elaborate. A military commitment to an indefinite stay at York was made about AD 120 when the original fortress was refortified and rebuilt internally in stone, and the surrounding area became fossilized as a permanent part of the settlement beside the fortress.

Knowledge of this part of Roman York is very patchy and inadequate, and there has been only a handful of small archaeological excavations and observations whose main contribution to understanding the area has been to show that it was laid out on a network of streets running at an angle to the adjacent fortress. More information about the buildings which stood in this vicinity has come from chance discoveries of inscribed or sculptured stones, which indicate that several temples stood here. These stone buildings belong to a time when the area was a well-established part of York, but there has been no trace of the earliest timber buildings. Coppergate provided a rare opportunity to examine a large part of the Roman civilian settlement, to trace it from its origins right through the three and a half centuries of Roman rule, and to see what

12 Foundation trenches for a Roman timber building showing as faint dark stains against the natural soil. Scale measures 50cm.

13 Foundation trenches for Roman timber building after excavation. Scale measures 50cm.

influence it had on the succeeding Anglo-Saxon and Viking Age city.

Being at the bottom of the archaeological deposits, the Roman layers were, of course, reached last, and although one tantalising fragment of Roman wall had been visible in the base of a later pit since quite early in the dig, it was not until 1980–1 that the main body of Roman structures was gradually uncovered. Even then, shortage of time and money meant that Roman levels were not exposed everywhere, but the southern half of the site was fully excavated, as was a strip across the Coppergate street frontage (11). The earliest remains were the foundations of timber buildings, showing up as trenches and gullies filled with a slightly darker soil than the naturally deposited yellow clay. In contrast with the later periods virtually no timber survived from these buildings, despite the soil being moist. The explanation for this is probably that the general standard of cleanliness within and around the Roman buildings was much higher than at any succeeding period up to the nineteenth century, and that a basic requirement for preservation is the rapid accumulation of organic-based domestic refuse like that which characterises the Viking Age and medieval occupation levels.

14 Foundation trenches for Roman timber buildings, cut into natural soil. Scale measures 1m.

15 Roman stone building, cut away by later pits. Scales measure 2m.

Over much of the area where Roman layers were reached, post-Roman pits and wells and later Roman stone buildings had destroyed quite large blocks of the earliest Roman levels, and not one complete plan of a timber building was recovered. The most coherent wooden structure lay in the northern corner of the site, where, after much careful trowelling, three parallel trenches each 60cm wide, up to 35cm deep and up to 4.6m long were recognised and excavated (12, 13). These might have held either horizontal foundation beams or a series of upright posts, or even a mixture of both elements, supporting a raised floor, but with no timbers surviving either intact or even as decayed stains in the soil, and with no impressions in the bases of the trenches, it is impossible to be certain which is the correct interpretation. Pottery fragments found amongst the soil backfill of these trenches are of types which were current in the few decades immediately after the Roman army's arrival in York, and they therefore suggest that the building was erected before *c.* AD 100.

As for the building's function, informed speculation and analysis of the environmental evidence from the trenches is the only approach, for no floor

levels survived and no diagnostic objects were recovered. Certainly the technique of fairly closely spaced foundation trenches is known to have been regularly used in warehouse construction, particularly for granaries where a raised floor supported by frequently spaced timbers was essential if the stored products were to be protected from damp and vermin. If the soil in the trenches got there when the building was dismantled, it may contain traces of plants, seeds or grain which were stored there, or perhaps remains of insects, usually beetles, which only live under certain very specific types of condition and which, if they are found in large quantities, may provide indirect evidence for what was stored inside. Only future research on the environmental samples from the three trenches may clarify these problems, but they have been described to give some idea of the problems of interpretation which confront the excavating archaeologist day by day.

16 Another view of the Roman stone building seen in 14, here represented mainly by foundation trenches (bounded by the dashed lines), and cut by Anglian and Viking Age features. Scales measure 2m.

ABOVE
17 Roman grave, cut away at left by a ninth-century pit, with the decayed wooden coffin showing as a dark streak. Scale measures 50cm.

Remains of other Roman timber buildings were also found in the southern half of the site, where a series of almost intercutting parallel trenches can be interpreted as the foundations of a succession of buildings (14). Their limits were either inaccessible beyond the site's perimeter piling, or were destroyed by later pits, and once again few recognisable floor layers survived. Thus, apart from noting

their alignment, which was at an angle both to the fortress and to the later medieval layout, and suggesting that they too were first built in about AD 100, there is little to say about them at present. They did not extend eastwards beyond a ditch which bisected the excavated area from north-east to south-west and which may have been a property division (11).

Eventually stone buildings replaced the timber ones in the south of the site, in some areas obliterating the slight remains of the timber-phase foundation trenches. For most of their extent the lines of the stone walls were as ghost-like as the timber buildings, because all the stonework, foundations included, had been thoroughly dismantled and removed for re-use (robbed) at some time before AD 920. Only three short lengths of limestone rubble wall survived, underpinned by substantial founda-

tions of alternating layers of stiff clay and cobbles. To these could be added the outline of other trenches extending for over thirty metres and outlining either a building of several rooms or an enclosure which occupied the lower part of the natural terrace above the River Foss (15, 16). Again no floor levels survived, and so only inference will suggest what function the building served.

The pottery from the Roman levels includes types which are known to have been current in the latest

ABOVE
18 Two pairs of *calcei*, hob-nailed shoes, from which the leather has rotted, at the feet of a Roman skeleton.

OPPOSITE
19 The Roman cremation urn, its stone lid still in place, lodged in the side of a Viking Age pit. Scale measures 20cm.

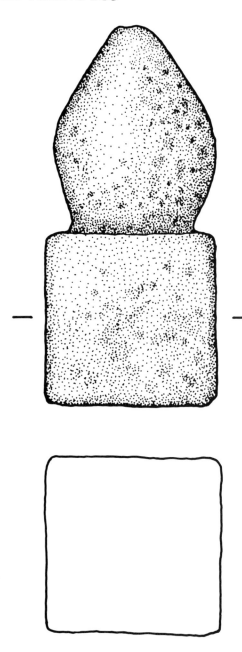

20 Gritstone finial from a Roman mausoleum. Height 73cm.

periods of Roman occupation in York, about AD 400, and so it seems that this area was in use until, with the breakdown of the Romano-British economy, town life began to disintegrate in the fifth century. It is not certain, however, that the Roman buildings were still occupied right up to *c*. 400 — it is possible that they had fallen into disuse before then, with the founding of a cemetery which occupied land near the Coppergate street frontage (11).

A scatter of half a dozen graves, on varying alignments, contained skeletons which in some cases lay in the badly decayed remains of wooden coffins (17). Generally the bodies had been laid out on their backs, with hands meeting above the pelvis, and with nothing buried to accompany them into the next world. In one, however, a string of beads was found around the neck, and in another two pairs of shoes had been placed in the coffin near the occupant's feet (18). None of the leather survived, but both pairs had hob-nails, a common Roman feature showing that they were *calcei*, a normal type of footwear in Roman Britain. The nails had kept their original relative positions in the soil, and with most careful trowelling the outlines of the shoes were revealed. The practice of burying footwear, perhaps to assist the deceased in the long walk into the next world, was widespread in Roman Britain, but normally one pair was thought sufficient to achieve whatever the purpose was. Why this man needed two pairs we can only guess.

More evidence for the nature of the cemetery came in the form of a single cremation urn, miraculously intact and with its stone lid still in place, embedded in the side of a Viking Age pit (19). There was also a large gritstone block, 73cm tall, looking like a pineapple perched on top of a cube, which was probably part of the capping decoration on a mausoleum which itself lay beyond the limits of the excavation (20). Although there was no evidence surviving around the graves to show that they had ever been marked in any way, a small fragment of a limestone slab, which originally had an inscription carved on it, was probably a memorial stone (21).

The skeletons from the cemetery are themselves

21 Fragmentary Roman tombstone. Height 15cm.

of great interest, for careful study reveals a great deal about their physique, life expectancy, diseases and disabilities. Three of them form a particularly unusual group, recognised because although the state of their joints and teeth indicates clearly that they were young adults in the 17–25 age group, all three skulls show characteristics of people very much older. This suggests that they form a family group, sharing this inherited genetic peculiarity, and may also indicate that there was at least one family plot in the cemetery. Such a small group cannot be used to generalise about the Romano-British population of York in the way that other much larger groups from the cemetery of St Helen-on-the-Walls in Aldwark have told us about the Viking Age and medieval inhabitants of a poor York parish, but they are welcome as a small contribution to the steadily growing number of carefully investigated Roman burials from York.

Apart from the grave-goods, there are remarkably few Roman objects of special interest from the site. Indeed, the two outstanding Roman objects were both found in layers of later periods — they got there through being dug up in the course of pit-digging, and thus being accidentally re-deposited in a layer of later date. One is a fragment of a clay tile,

27

distinguished from all the other tens of thousands of tile fragments dug up at Coppergate by the fact that the tile-maker scratched a message into the wet clay before it was fired (22). The shape and form of the letters is in cursive script, the free-running everyday handwriting style of the period. Unfortunately the surviving fragment is so small that this message from the past cannot be deciphered.

The second notable Roman small find is a tiny oval gem-stone of carnelian, only 19mm long, which served as a seal in a signet-ring (23). The stone is engraved with a beautifully executed miniature design of a charioteer in full flight, whipping on a pair of horses which pull the two-wheeled chariot. The figure has been identified as Cupid, who was quite a popular choice as a personal device or motif on intaglios such as this.

The young countryman from the Yorkshire Dales, visiting York for the first time *c*. AD 100, would have been astonished to see buildings on a scale and in such a density as he had never seen before. The structures were made of timber, recently erected to serve the needs of the Roman IX Legion, whose fortress, with its earth rampart topped by a wooden palisade, was visible on the slightly higher ground to the north-west, one hundred and fifty metres away. Down on the River Foss small boats were unloading supplies and raw materials, and the place was bustling with merchants, entrepreneurs, craftsmen, traders and off-duty soldiers. Already rebuilding was in progress, as some of the earliest buildings erected when the legion first moved to York in AD *c*.71 were being replaced. For the local people, it was a new world, but while many of them resented the imposition of martial law and longed again for independence, others were capitalising on the new trading opportunities and enjoying a higher standard of living than had been available previously.

Nine generations or so later, *c*. AD 350, this visitor's thoroughly Romanised descendant, standing on the same spot, would again have made out the legionary fortress in the middle distance, although by now it was the VI Legion which was stationed there, and the old earth-and-timber defences had long been replaced by a stone wall. Impressive stone or stone-and-timber buildings now partially masked the fortress from view and extended in places for some way down the slope towards the River Foss, but there were some open spaces too, and in one there was a small cemetery, with most of the graves marked by low mounds but also some with more elaborate funeral monuments. The area was still as busy as ever, and there seemed no reason to think that things would not continue in the same prosperous vein for centuries to come. For this visitor's grandson, however, all this hustle and bustle would have been only a childhood recollection—within a short time the Roman army and its attendant prosperity would leave York for good.

22 Fragmentary inscribed Roman tile. Length 6.9cm.

3
The Elusive Angles

The two hundred years following the withdrawal of the VI Legion back to Italy *c.* AD 400 are the most mysterious in all of York's history, with few written records to provide a historical framework, and little archaeological material to fill the gap. Just south of the city at the Mount and to the north at Heworth, small cemeteries of easily identifiable cremation urns dated to the fifth/sixth century show that immigrants from North Germany and Denmark, Angles and Saxons, were in the vicinity then, but there is virtually no evidence for them within the city itself.

Only with the conversion to Christianity of Edwin, the Anglo-Saxon king of Northumbria, and his baptism in York in 627, did the city again become a place of interest to the small literate community in contemporary England, the Church. Edwin (616–32) was acknowledged as Bretwalda, the most prestigious among contemporary Anglo-Saxon kings, and this title was also accorded to his successors Oswald (634–42) and Oswy (642–70). Northumbrian power was at its zenith in the seventh and eighth centuries, and this period was also one of great intellectual, artistic and academic achievement, inspired by twin sources, the Celtic Church of Ireland and Scotland, and the papal mission whose contacts extended across Europe to Rome. In liturgical matters the Roman Church, which was responsible for Edwin's baptism, was to triumph, but the artistic achievements of the Celtic Church

are known to us through masterpieces such as the illuminated manuscript called the Lindisfarne Gospels. Irish scholarship too was renowned in western Europe, but the Northumbrian adherents to the Roman Church soon acquired books, relics and practical skills such as architecture from the Church on the continent, particularly from Rome, and established their own reputation for learning.

The story of this Golden Age of Northumbrian Christianity is known partly through the writings of Bede (*c.* 672–735), a monk at the twin monasteries of Wearmouth/Jarrow, who recorded the establishment of the bishopric at York in 627, and the founding of a monastic school. This flourished in the eighth century, and one of its scholars, the priest Alcuin (730–804), was summoned by Charles the Great, founder of the Carolingian Empire, to take charge of his palace schools. The intellectual importance of York at this time is undoubted, but even so, contemporary written references to the city are very meagre. They tell us mainly of the names of kings, bishops and archbishops, of the building of churches and a monastery in York, then called Eoforwic, and in passing of the presence of a community of traders from the Low Countries at the end of the eighth century.

Archaeological finds to flesh out the historical skeleton of the royal, ecclesiastical and mercantile centre are almost non-existent. Excavations undertaken by the York Minster Archaeology Office have

shown that the Roman headquarters building, now partly buried below the nave of York Minster, seems to have stood intact and in use throughout this Anglian period. It was probably in royal ownership, and perhaps formed the nucleus of a palace complex with the cathedral church nearby. Whatever its function, it represents nearly all we know about Anglian York, whose archaeology remains notoriously elusive.

We had hoped that above the Roman layers at Coppergate there would be remains of the Anglo-Saxon period—in particular, as a riverside site, it seemed entirely appropriate that there might be some trace of mercantile settlement. Instead, a layer of sterile grey soil varying from a few millimetres to over 50cm in thickness covered the latest Roman remains described in the previous chapter, and represents the period between the end of Roman occupation c. AD 400 and the beginning of Scandinavian settlement more than four hundred and fifty

24 Part of a Roman building and adjacent debris from its collapse covered by the sterile, uniform soil which built up during the Anglian period. Scale measures 50cm.

years later (24). Even the most careful trowelling and a willingness to investigate the most unconvincing suspicions of archaeological features failed to reveal much evidence for Anglian activity on the site in this period, and the grey soil seems to result from the gradual accumulation of natural deposits transported to the site by wind and water without any human interference. This picture of abandonment is reinforced by the study of the animal remains from this period: there was a great diversity of small mammal species, including the common shrew, water shrew and field vole, which do not generally live alongside man.

The only substantial features which could possibly belong to this period are a mysterious curving

30

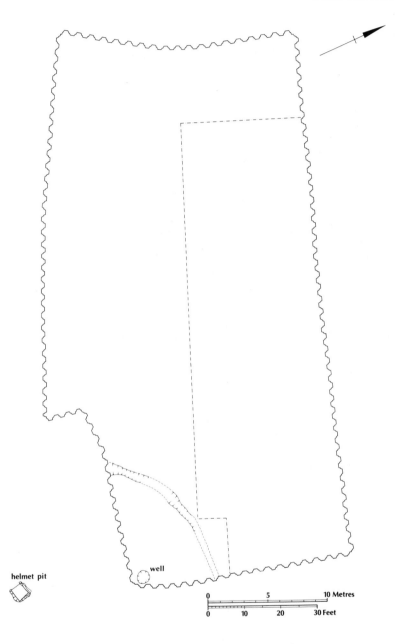

helmet pit

well

0   5   10 Metres

0   10   20   30 Feet

25 The Coppergate site during the Anglian period, *c.* 400–850, and the position of the wood-lined shaft containing the Coppergate helmet. The featureless area between the dashed line and the shoring in the north-east part of the site was not investigated at this depth.

ABOVE
27 A well-shaft of the Anglian period, made by
hollowing out a length of black poplar tree trunk.
Scale measures 50cm.

OPPOSITE
23 Roman gem stone engraved with a charioteer
(p. 28). Length 1.9cm.

28 Anglian period *stycas*, the debased coinage of
pre-Viking Northumbria, with a half new penny as a
comparative scale.

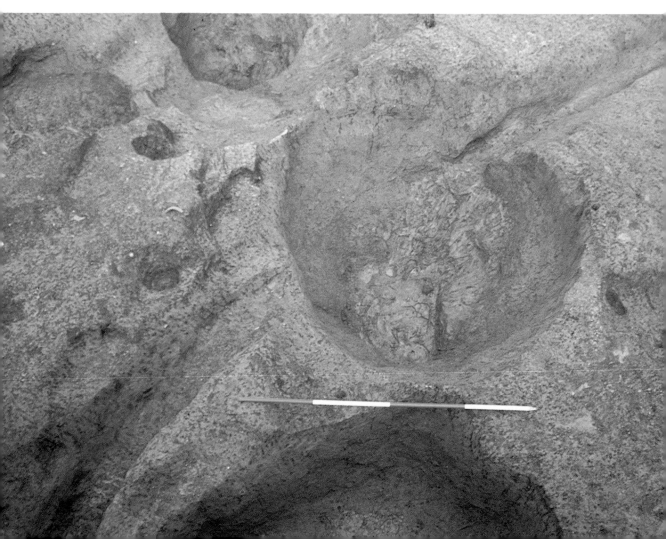

ditch or gulley in the south-east corner of the site, enclosing a space which had a well-shaft within it (25). Both the gulley and the well were dug into the main structure of Roman date, part of a lengthy stone building (above p. 23), and seem to be broadly contemporary with its dismantling. Unfortunately the dating of these two features is only approximate, since all the pottery found in them is of Roman types. Although this superficially suggests that the features themselves are Roman, groups of pure Roman pottery are also the normal pattern in Anglian period layers in York, for remarkably little domestic pottery of the Anglian period has been found in the city. There was, however, no Viking Age pottery in these features, and this would almost certainly have been present if they had been dug after about AD 850–75. This negative evidence therefore, coupled with the stratigraphic position of these features, sandwiched between Roman and Viking Age levels, indicates that they do belong to the Anglian period.

It is difficult to interpret the purpose of the gulley (26). Its sides were vertical, showing no sign of the erosion which would be expected if it had stood open; the soil filling it was hardly distinguished from the soil into which it was cut; and there was no indication in the form of mortar, laid stones, timber or even impressions where timber once stood that it had held any of these possible elements. While it remains most likely that it defined part of a building or enclosure, at present it remains enigmatic.

The well within the arc was unique on the site in having a lining made from a hollowed length of the trunk of a black poplar tree (27). This lining had been placed into a circular well-shaft which had itself been reinforced with a wattle support to prevent its collapse. This wattle may eventually provide an approximate date for the well's construction by means of a carbon-14 analysis, but at present

OPPOSITE
29 Blue glass and silver stud of the Anglian period. Diameter 1.4cm.
26 Curving gulley of the Anglian period, cut by a Viking Age pit. Scale measures 2m.

it can only be said to date c. 400–850. Yet despite this uncertainty over dating, both well and gulley are of interest in showing that within this shadowy period of York's development there was some sort of activity here beside the River Foss. Several other pits in the immediate vicinity which also contained only Roman pottery, but seem to have been dug from above the Roman levels, corroborate this impression.

In addition to these few features only a handful of 'small finds' belonging to the Anglian period were discovered in the excavation. They included a small number of Northumbrian stycas, the debased silver coins minted in York by the Northumbrian kings and archbishops (28). These only circulated north of the Humber, for they were already out of date in the other more southerly English kingdoms where the higher quality and larger silver penny had been adopted as the unit of currency. The stycas excavated at Coppergate may not have been lost on the site; they may have been found elsewhere by later occupants, who brought them home as curiosities, just as Roman coins too must sometimes have been picked up and kept. Great numbers of stycas were in circulation in the eighth and early ninth centuries—a hoard containing ten thousand was found in York in 1840—and they must have been reasonably well known to later inhabitants.

This explanation might account also for a much more unusual Anglo-Saxon object, a blue glass stud in a simply ornamented silver setting with two small prongs protruding from its rear face (29). These prongs would have been pushed through and folded behind the larger object in whose decorative scheme the stud formed only one small element, and a remarkable survival has given us an indication of what this larger object might have been. At some unknown date before 1823, in Ormside churchyard in Cumberland, a grave-digger found a decorated bronze bowl which is now one of the treasures of the Yorkshire Museum, and one of England's finest surviving examples of Anglo-Saxon craftsmanship in metalwork. It bears a series of designs beaten into the metal, which include interlaced plant motifs and fantastic animals whose ancestry can be traced to

THE VIKING DIG

classical forms. Their style here suggests that the bowl was made about AD 800. The bowl is further embellished both inside and out with studs virtually identical to the one found at Coppergate, and although this does not mean that the Coppergate stud was made for a similar bowl, there is a chance that this was so.

This was the sum total of Anglian period objects recognised in the Coppergate excavation and, like the structural remains of the period, they were of interest, but in all, perhaps, rather a disappointment. This feeling was, however, completely overturned by one remarkable discovery made only nine metres beyond the edge of the archaeological excavation during construction work in 1982. This discovery was made thanks to a fortunate combination of circumstances and shows that even in these days of scientific methods the archaeologist needs good luck and ceaseless vigilance. In effect, the discovery was an undreamt of archaeological bonus, but it was also a supreme justification of the policy, adopted by York Archaeological Trust and funded by the Department of the Environment, which kept a small team of archaeologists on the site during the redevelopment, to record whatever buildings and objects were brought to light in the contractor's large-scale earth-moving operations. The site's developers, Messrs Wimpey, gave total co-operation in this watching brief, which soon settled into a routine of monitoring and measuring. This was rewarded with the salvaging of information about the medieval waterfront of the River Foss and further details of Viking Age and Roman remains to supplement the information gained during the excavation proper. But the most exciting find came near the end of the watching brief, when the outline of the new building covering the excavation site and its surrounds had been finalised.

Last-minute alterations in design had included the abandoning of plans for a double basement at one point, and the substitution of a single basement instead. Most of the area involved had been mechanically excavated to single-basement depth some months previously, and then left open until final planning decisions were taken. Now all that

remained to be done was a last scraping over of the area by a machine to make it approximately level, and then to cover it with stone chippings to provide a firm base for the building work. A huge mechanical digger was used for the scraping over, with its driver, perched in his cab about ten metres from the extended bucket, being directed by a 'ganger' standing in front. Pure routine . . . until the ganger spotted that the bucket had hit what at first he thought was a piece of stone, possibly a remnant of the massive brick chimney of Craven's sweet factory which had formerly stood just here, with its foundations descending to within a few centimetres of the new basement level. Signalling the driver to stop, he went and had a closer look—and realised that the obstruction was not stone but metal, mostly rusty brown in colour but also with strips that looked like gold. One part had been dislodged by the machine and the surrounding area slightly buckled, but the object seemed largely intact. He ran his finger along the golden strip, and saw letters stamped on it. Clearly this was something unusual and so, leaving the object half buried in the ground, he called over one of the archaeologists.

What they had found was a helmet, recognisable by its general outline which could be seen even though three-quarters of the face was still buried, and by one hinged cheek-guard which was clearly visible. Helmets of any date are extremely rare finds, and within a short time a small team of archaeologists had gathered to ensure its safe removal and the retrieval of the maximum amount of information about how it came to be lying there. Wimpey immediately agreed to suspend work in the area, and gave all possible assistance.

A trowelling of the helmet's immediate surrounds showed that it was lying inside a 90cm-square wooden shaft which had been sunk into the natural yellow clay (30). Only the bottom 20cm of this frame survived—everything above had been sliced away by the chimney foundations and the contractor's machines. The helmet was lying in soil that was mostly sticky clay, and similar clay had filled its interior. This had helped to preserve its shape and to conserve the metal itself, for a watertight and

30 The Coppergate helmet lying in the wood-lined pit where it was discovered. Scale measures 50cm.

airtight layer of clay is one of the best archaeological preservatives there is—in Norway, Viking Age ships have been found virtually complete, sealed below such clay. The clay clung to the helmet, and increased the difficulties of lifting it. This, however, could not be hurried—plans had to be drawn, photographs taken, and the remainder of the shaft carefully excavated to see if anything else lay within it. During this work more of the helmet was gradually exposed, and an initial impression that it was of Anglo-Saxon date, c. AD 600–800, was confirmed as more details became visible. Particu-

larly characteristic were the long nose guard or nasal, and the eyebrows, which had a stylised animal head between them and other smaller animal heads in profile at their ends. This preliminary dating made the find still more exciting, for only two other helmets of this date have been found in England. Both came from aristocratic or royal burials—one, surviving only as an iron framework, dug up in 1848

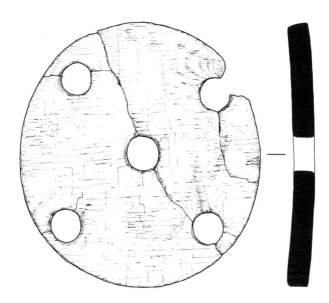

in a grave mound at Benty Grange in the Peak District of Derbyshire (now in Sheffield City Museum), and the other, richly decorated but fragmentary, excavated in 1939 from the royal ship burial at Sutton Hoo in Suffolk (now in the British Museum).

These, and most of the contemporary examples from Scandinavia and other parts of Europe, had been buried as grave-goods, but clearly the Coppergate helmet was not a burial deposit—the shaft was not long enough to receive a skeleton, and there was no evidence for a cremation deposit—no cremation urn, for example. The purpose of the shaft is not yet known, and may never be, although scientific analysis of soil from within it has indicated that the shaft was cut in the open air and surrounded with weeds before it was filled in. One thing at least is certain; it was not a cesspit. Why the helmet was left in the shaft will probably remain a mystery. It seems unlikely that it was thrown away—it is in such good condition and anyway had a value as scrap or re-usable metal. Could it have represented looted or stolen goods, hastily disposed of to avoid detection?

During the helmet's excavation several other objects were found in the shaft, including Roman

31 Perforated wooden disc from the wood-lined shaft containing the Coppergate Anglian helmet. Diameter 13.2cm.

pottery, slag, and a perforated wooden disc (31), but the only one which was almost certainly put in the shaft deliberately with the helmet is a long slender iron spearhead which can also be positively identified as Anglo-Saxon (32). It was lying against one side of the shaft, slightly bent, most probably by pressure of soil accumulating above.

Eventually, as darkness fell five hours after the helmet first came to light, the excavation of the shaft was completed and the helmet was eased from its resting place and taken away to safe-keeping. As it was lifted a good deal of bated breath was gently expelled, for it seemed in remarkably good condition; and just visible within it were traces of a cheek-piece and a mail neck-guard. All the soil excavated from the shaft was kept for fine sorting and scientific analysis, and in addition soil from the area around which the machine had moved immediately before the discovery was also bagged up and removed, in the hope of recovering any small fragments which the machine had knocked off.

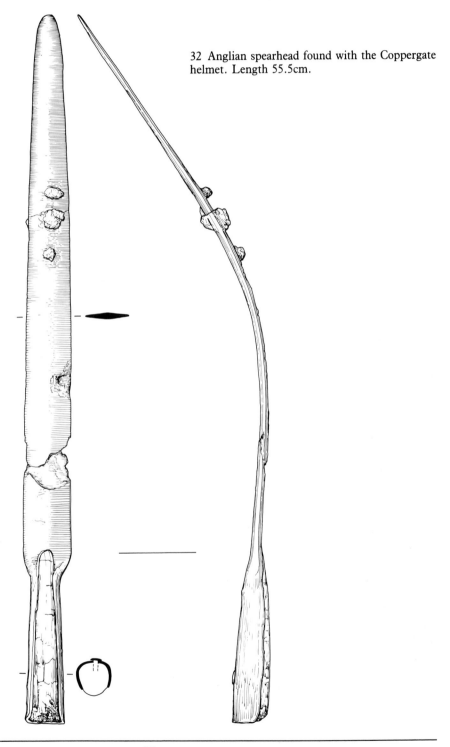

32 Anglian spearhead found with the Coppergate helmet. Length 55.5cm.

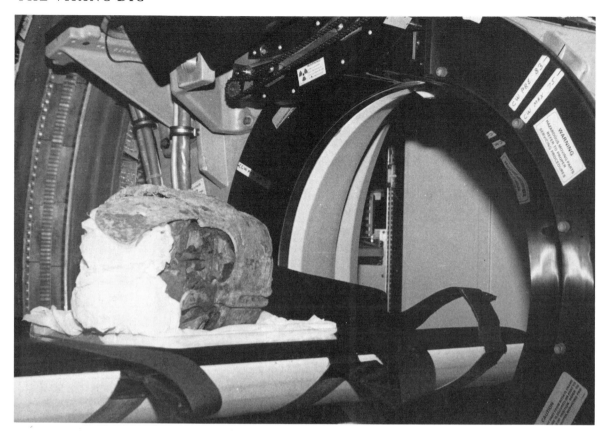

33 The Coppergate helmet being examined with the aid of York District Hospital's body scanner.

The cleaning of the helmet was undertaken by York Archaeological Trust's conservators after a preliminary programme which included x-rays and computer tomography using York District Hospital's body scanner (33). Tomograms are x-rays which isolate a single layer through their subject at a predetermined point—in this case a series of tomograms through the helmet enabled the positions of the mail and second cheek-piece, still buried within it, to be plotted with accuracy before cleaning commenced (34). Following the painstaking conservation work, the technical mastery of the helmet's construction and the magnificence of its decoration are now revealed (**35**, pp. 48–9).

The helmet consists of four main elements. Its framework is made up of a broad band of iron encircling the head, the brow-band, to which is riveted another band running from front to back over the crown. This in turn is attached to the brow-band by two shorter bands, running over the ears and also riveted into position. The four spaces between these various bands are filled by sub-triangular iron plates, once again held in place by rivets. The wearer probably protected his head and ears from the chafing of the metal by donning a leather or woollen cap before pulling the helmet on, but this seems to have been a separate item of headgear since no trace of any such protective lining remained within the helmet.

Two iron flaps, hinged to the helmet, protected the cheeks, and could be tied in place below the chin. The back of the neck was defended by a length

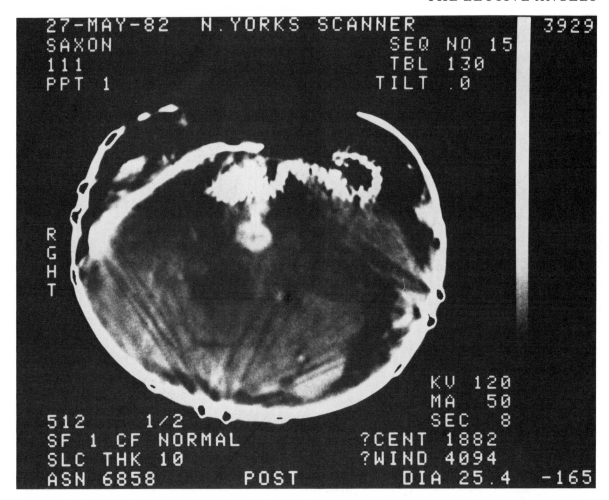

```
27-MAY-82   N.YORKS SCANNER            3929
SAXON                     SEQ NO 15
111                       TBL 130
PPT 1                     TILT .0

R
G
H
T

                                        KV 120
                                        MA  50
                                        SEC  8
512        1/2
SF 1 CF NORMAL            ?CENT 1882
SLC THK 10               ?WIND 4094
ASN 6858        POST      DIA 25.4   -165
```

of iron mail, suspended from the lower edge of the brow-band and attached to the rear edges of the cheek-pieces to form a curtain of mail. Although concreted together with rust when found, cleaning the mail has restored its complete flexibility and allowed its detailed study. It consists of two thousand individual iron links, and is in itself a testimony to the skill of the Anglian smith (36, 37).

The brow-band had two semi-circles cut from it to form eye holes, and these are decorated with brass edging to form eyebrows, embellished with a hatched design and terminating at either outer end in snarling, stylised animal heads (38). There is also a brass edging strip around the lower edge of the

34 Tomogram of the Coppergate helmet showing the mail neck-guard and second cheek-piece as lighter areas towards top right and from upper centre to centre left respectively: the light circular area at centre was a stone.

brow-band and around the cheek-pieces. The eyebrows run together and downward to form a nose-guard or nasal, which is itself decorated with two interlaced animals (frontispiece 1a). This decoration is preserved in such fine condition that on closer inspection even the laying-out lines, made by its designer when he carved the original master-mould into wood before casting the brass

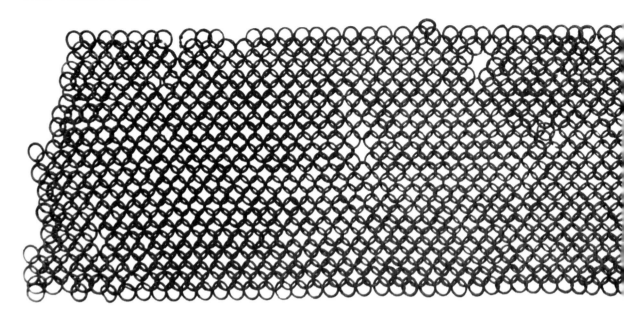

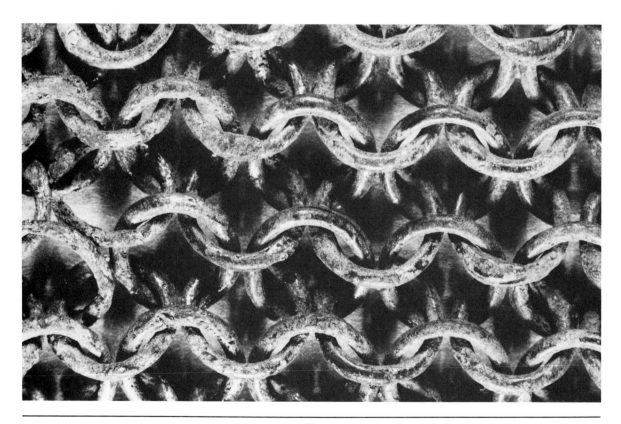

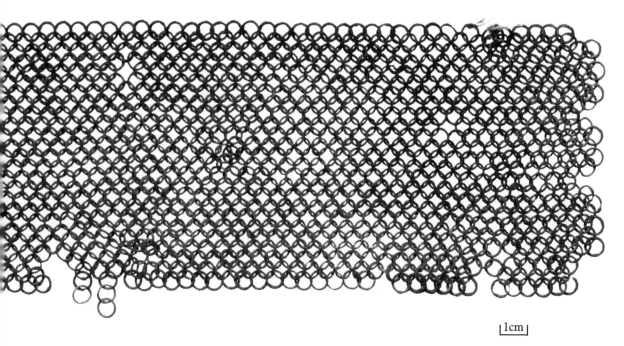

⌊1cm⌋

ABOVE
36 Mail neck-guard from the Coppergate helmet after conservation.

OPPOSITE
37 Detail of the interlinked mail neck-guard from the Coppergate helmet.

nasal, are visible. Between the eyebrows is another animal head shown as if seen from above, with an extended, rounded muzzle, large eyes and incised shapes representing flattened ears. This animal head forms the end of raised twin decorative ridges, extending from nose to nape, which hold in place a brass strip bearing an inscription in letters that were hammered into relief from underneath.

The inscription is mainly in Latin, and incorporates several standard abbreviations (39). Supplying the missing letters in brackets, it reads:

IN. NOMINE. D(omi)NI. NOSTRI. IH(s)U(s). S(an)C(tu)S. SP(iritu)S. D(e)I. ET. OMNIBUS. DECEMUS. AMEN. OSHERE.

The inscription ends with the Greek letters XPI, the first three letters of the Greek spelling of the name of Christ. This can be freely translated as

'In the name of our Lord Jesus, the Holy Spirit, God and with all we pray. Amen. Oshere. Christ.'

It seems to be a prayer invoking protection for the helmet's wearer. At right angles to this inscription is another, running from ear to ear, but interrupted by the first inscription. Although damaged where struck by the mechanical digger, this bipartite inscription seems to have been identical to the first. The opening words of its two halves were positioned above the brow-band on either side, and thus the prayer does not make sense when the inscription is read straight across from one ear to the other. This

41

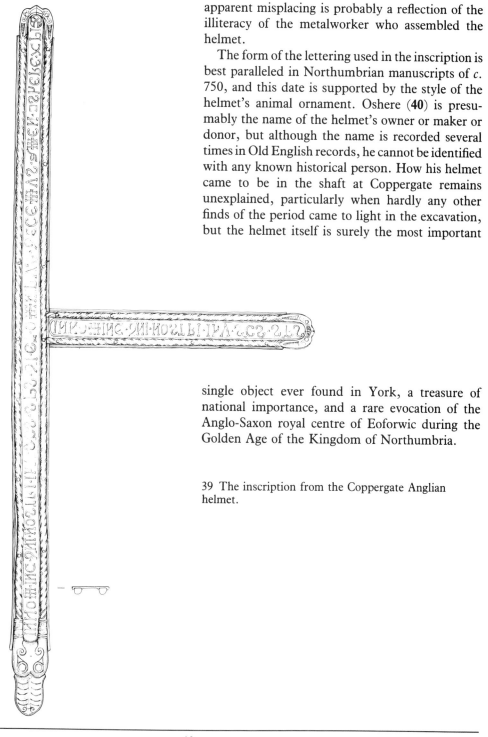

apparent misplacing is probably a reflection of the illiteracy of the metalworker who assembled the helmet.

The form of the lettering used in the inscription is best paralleled in Northumbrian manuscripts of *c.* 750, and this date is supported by the style of the helmet's animal ornament. Oshere (**40**) is presumably the name of the helmet's owner or maker or donor, but although the name is recorded several times in Old English records, he cannot be identified with any known historical person. How his helmet came to be in the shaft at Coppergate remains unexplained, particularly when hardly any other finds of the period came to light in the excavation, but the helmet itself is surely the most important

single object ever found in York, a treasure of national importance, and a rare evocation of the Anglo-Saxon royal centre of Eoforwic during the Golden Age of the Kingdom of Northumbria.

39 The inscription from the Coppergate Anglian helmet.

4
New Impetus -
the Viking Arrival

Alcuin had only just taken up his post with Charles the Great when he learned of a Viking attack on the island monastery at Lindisfarne, off the Northumbrian coast, in 793. This attack marks the beginning of the Viking Age in Western Europe. In England a series of hit and run raids aimed at rich and principally undefended targets, notably the monasteries, gave way in 865 to the start of an extended campaign by a Viking army permanently based in England, in which three of the four main English kingdoms were eventually defeated and their lands settled by Scandinavian immigrants.

York was the first target for this 'great army' as it was called by the English. After landing in Kent in 865, the Vikings marched to York in 866 and captured the city with relative ease—the Northumbrians were divided by civil war, which must have hampered their defensive measures. Nonetheless they regrouped into a united front to counterattack the Viking army in York in 867, but were soundly beaten with severe loss of life. From this time the Vikings held the city almost without interruption until 954, and in 876 part of the Viking 'great army' settled in and around York, which they called Jorvik, making it the capital of the Viking kingdom of York, and devoting an increasing amount of their energies to agriculture, industry and trade rather than to warfare.

The archaeological evidence from the excavation agrees with and amplifies the historical picture. In the years c. 850–900 the area saw activity on a scale unknown since the last days of the Roman era, with a glass-making furnace marking the start of manufacturing here. This may have been before the Viking invasion of 866—after the furnace fell into disuse, the area around it was used for waste disposal in pits. A few of the pits contained human skeletons, perhaps victims of the Viking take-over; others contained domestic debris, and by now there must have been people living very close by, if not actually on the site. New properties were marked out by wooden fences, and perhaps the street which we know as Coppergate was established. This was the start of a new era of expansion.

The layer of grey soil which seems to represent the virtual desertion of the Coppergate site during the Anglian period was covered by a series of layers which, although much the same in colour, were differentiated by the presence of many fairly easily recognisable features (41). These were distinguishable through being slightly different in colour or texture from the uniform grey soil, and were of four main types.

Firstly there was evidence for industry on the site at this period. The base of a kiln or furnace, recognisable as an area of re-used Roman tiles surrounded by soil which had been baked to a red colour, was partially enclosed by shallow trenches in which its walls had once stood (42). A date for the furnace's use has been calculated using archaeo-

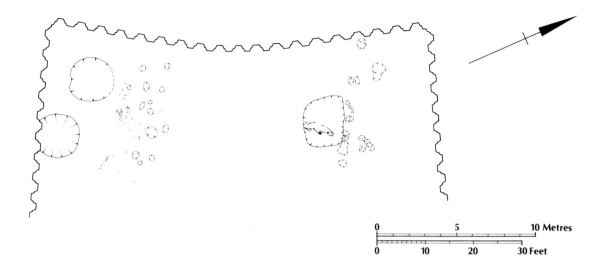

41 The Coppergate site during the period of Viking settlement, c. 850–900. Features of this era were found only at the Coppergate end of the excavation: for the extent of the site investigated at this depth see illustration 25.

magnetic dating techniques. The principles of this are relatively simple and are based on the fact that the direction of the Earth's magnetic field at a particular place changes with time. Any archaeological feature which becomes magnetised by the Earth's magnetic field at the time of its formation and which is found undisturbed can be dated by comparing its direction of magnetism with an established magnetic curve master chart. Most soils and clays include small percentages of the minerals magnetite and haematite which themselves contain iron, and when kilns or furnaces are in use the high temperatures cause these minerals in the surrounding soil or in the bricks and tiles of the furnace to lose their original magnetisation and then, as they cool, to become re-magnetised by the Earth's magnetic field. It is this new magnetic field which, when measured and compared with the master chart, provides a date for the last firing of the furnace. The date arrived at for this Coppergate furnace was c. AD 860, a date which fits well with the relative position of the furnace in the overall build-up of layers.

On the furnace's periphery a small cache of about thirty glass fragments was found, suggesting that the furnace was connected with glass-working in some form (43). They included pieces which were unmistakably Roman in origin, and which had been collected for re-melting—such recycled glass is known as cullet. Other pieces, looking like narrow, bent rods, are typical of the residue from glass-making, and had also been carefully gathered up for re-use. More evidence that helps to identify the methods used by the glassworkers was not recognised until some months after the first piece of it was dug up. This was because it was pottery of a type unlike anything seen before (44, 45, pp. 64–5). When shown to Roman pottery experts they suggested it was medieval, post-medieval or even modern, while experts on these later periods held that it was either Roman or 'exotic', perhaps Near Eastern. Near Eastern pottery experts disowned it.

This baffling pottery sometimes had a red outer coating, occasionally burnished with a decoration of wavy lines, applied to a clay which was fired to a creamy colour. Most of the vessels are jars with a prominent rolled-over rim. Their shape, colour and decoration all pointed to a Roman date, but this seemed to be ruled out by the fact that many of the pieces were covered or partially covered, both inside and out, with a clear glaze that gave them a brownish-coloured appearance. With a few exceptions, the Romans did not produce glazed pottery in England, and certainly nothing like this—so what was it? A substantial clue came when an almost complete base sherd was found, on which the 'glaze' was approximately 1cm thick—a 'glassy' deposit rather than just a glaze, although both have the same chemical composition. Analysis at both the Department of the Environment's Ancient Monuments Laboratory in London and the Corning Museum of Glass in New York soon confirmed that this deposit was indeed a glass-making residue, and that previously unexplained patches and dribbles of encrustation on the rims and outsides of several pieces consisted of sand, a raw material in glass-making, which had only partially turned into glass.

Recognition that the jars were being used to hold molten glass accounts for the 'glaze', but still leaves unexplained the source and date of the pottery, since it is unlike any other known types of the later ninth century. However, it has been suggested that the pots were Roman in origin, originally used as cremation urns, and that when found by chance in the ninth century they were dug up and re-used because they were of much better quality than the contemporary pottery, and particularly suitable for industrial processes at high temperatures. York, with its large Roman population over several centuries, was flanked by extensive cemeteries including cremation urns. Thus they were readily available, and at present this seems to be the most likely explanation for these unusual pots, although the discovery of a Roman pottery kiln, abandoned with its last load of pots still in place, might also have provided a source for their supply. Refiring in the furnace would have altered the colour of the clay from the grey of the Roman period to the cream as it was discovered, and accounts for Roman pottery experts not recognising the vessels as Roman products.

Glassmaking is itself a rare discovery at this date in England, and historians of technology will thus await the results of further scientific analysis with interest. The Coppergate material should be an important index of the technical competence of late ninth-century glass-makers. Unfortunately, no evidence has yet been recognised for what they were making. Simple glass beads are most likely, but none were found in a half-finished or discarded condition, as normally happens at manufacturing sites. Window glass and glass vessels are other possibilities, although both are believed to have been rare at this period. All Saints' Church, just twenty metres away from the furnace, may have been built by this time and might perhaps have had glazed windows—but this is all conjecture.

The second use to which this area was put in the late ninth century was for human burials. When the furnace was no longer in operation, a square rubbish pit was dug into it and used to dispose of the corpse of an adult male aged twenty-five to thirty-five (46). The body had been interred on its back, but the left arm was bent with the hand below the head and the elbow cocked well above the rest of the body. This unlikely position of the arm had perhaps been maintained because the muscle stiffening, *rigor mortis*, was still having its effect when the body was buried, but the peculiar position of the left thigh bone and part of the pelvis is the result of later, accidental, disturbance. This was the only complete Viking Age human skeleton discovered, but the badly disturbed remains of several others were recorded in contemporary levels nearby. They are unusual because owing to their stratigraphic position they can be dated to the late ninth century, a precision not generally possible with Anglo-Saxon or Viking Age burials except for the few which were accompanied by coins. They thus provide a glimpse of York's population at this time. Their sex, age at death, physical attributes and any peculiarities of bone structure resulting from disease, diet or their occupation will all be identified. This data will then be compared with that from the much larger group of broadly contemporary citizens recovered before redevelopment of the cemetery of St Helen-on-the-Walls Church in Aldwark, some 400m away. The Aldwark group showed a population comparable in physique to people being examined for military

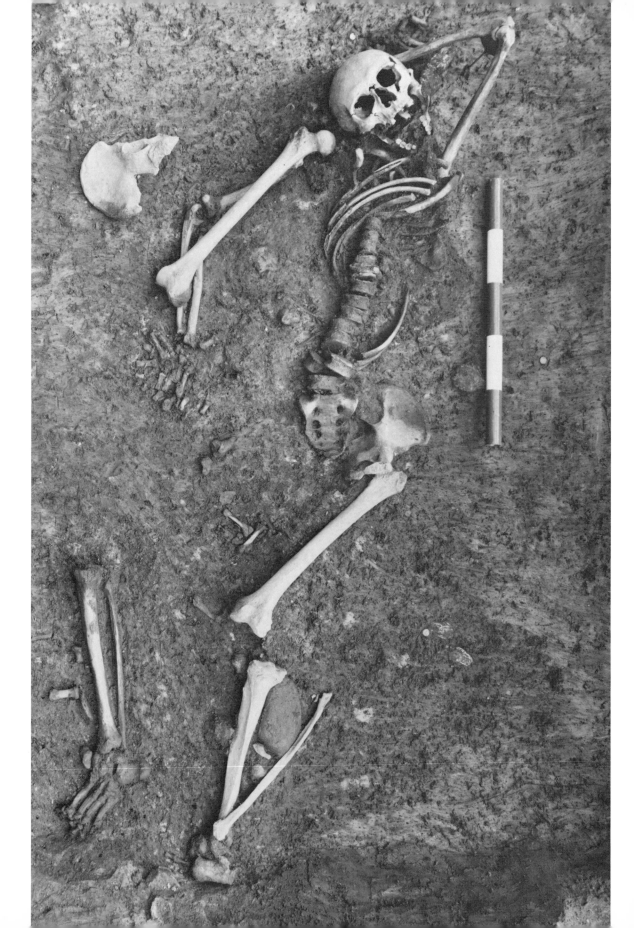

service in Britain during 1939–45, and the Coppergate skeletons will probably conform to this pattern. Life-span, however, was much less then than it is today: over a quarter of the population died in childhood, over half the adult women died before they were thirty-five, and only about one person in ten reached the age of sixty.

Three possible explanations of why these skeletons were buried at Coppergate suggest themselves. One is dependent upon the assumption that the nearby All Saints' Church was already in existence before AD 900. If this was so, then it is just conceivable that the burials were outliers from a cemetery around the church, but the rather haphazard disposal of the first body argues against this. Alternatively, it may be that the skeletons represent victims of war or civil disturbance, buried near where they fell. In the later ninth century there are at least three documented occasions which could have led to such burials—the Viking capture of York in 866, the disastrous Anglian counter-attack of 867 and an anti-Viking uprising of 872 which brought the Viking army back to the city to quash the dissidents. All may have been bloody affairs, but only the struggle in 867 is reported in a near contemporary source. The *Anglo-Saxon Chronicle* records that the Angles

'. . . collected a large army and attacked the enemy in York and broke into the city; and some of them got inside, and an immense slaughter was made of them, some inside and some outside . . .'

If one of these three events accounts for the skeletons, then the archaeomagnetic date centred on *c*. AD 860 for the glass-making furnace appears to fit quite well. There may also have been other unrecorded battles and brawls in York at this time, and these too could have left a number of bodies lying in the city. The least troublesome way of disposing of these afterwards would have been to bury them in convenient pits, and the lack of care and ceremony suggest that this 'tidying up' was done by the victors, not the vanquished. The principal objection to this explanation is that there does not seem to be any indication of violent death on the skeletons, although visible signs of foul play are not always obvious. A third possibility is that the burials are of Scandinavian settlers who had not yet adopted the local Christian Anglian custom of interring their dead in the city's churchyards. Yet this also is not totally convincing because Viking Age cemeteries in Scandinavia are usually more regularly arranged, and for the present these burials remain something of a mystery.

Thirdly, there were several large square or circular pits, up to 1.7m wide and approaching two metres in depth, which were backfilled with deposits of various types, amongst which a moist, smelly, brown or greenish-tinged brown silt was common. This was probably human cess, an identification which will be checked in the environmental laboratory, and it may be significant that from some of the pits containing this substance we also recovered textile fragments in relatively large numbers—could they have been used as toilet paper? The pits also contained quantities of animal bones and mollusc shells, which are interpreted as domestic food refuse, and pottery of both Roman and later dates. The Roman pieces are 'residual'—churned up from below in pit-digging—and were to recur in steadily diminishing amounts right through the medieval features. The later pottery was found in rather larger pieces than the Roman sherds, and this in itself would suggest that it had not been buried for so long and subjected to reworking of the soil with the consequent breakage into smaller and smaller fragments. It was recognised by its rough gritty texture and its characteristic shapes and colour as being what is known as 'York ware'. This pottery was first recognised as a distinct type during rescue excavations in the city in 1950–1, but it had to wait until the excavation at Lloyds Bank, 6–8 Pavement, in 1972–3 before its correct dating was first determined. There it was established as a type which appeared early in the Anglo-Scandinavian

OPPOSITE
46 Human skeleton, slightly disturbed at a later date, from an unceremonious late ninth-century burial—a victim of the Viking takeover? Scale measures 50cm.

period, i.e. in the period AD 850–900, and this relatively early date was confirmed by its position in the Coppergate sequence, where it first appeared in those features which were themselves buried beneath undisturbed layers closely dated by coins to the first decades of the tenth century. Several nearly complete York ware pots were recovered, and one of them could be totally reconstructed (47).

These features, which were easy to distinguish, lay within sub-divisions of the site which were much harder to pick out, but which are of considerable importance to our overall picture of the area's development, since they may be a first attempt to parcel out the land here into separately owned tenements. The divisions, the fourth component of the archaeology of this period, ran back from the present street frontage at a slight angle, and were represented not by surviving timbers but by circular stains marking the holes where posts had once stood. Although these post-holes seemed big enough to take building timbers for houses, and unnecessarily large for just a fence line, they did not form the rectangles or square outlines of buildings, but seem to have been straight lines. If they were indeed property boundaries, then it seems that individual plots were laid out very soon after the Scandinavian settlement. It is also possible that the street Coppergate became a regular thoroughfare at this time, although this is only speculation—the Viking Age street was much narrower than its modern namesake, and lies irretrievably buried beneath it. What is certain is that intensive occupation did not start until several decades after this first sub-division of the area, and Coppergate cannot be assumed to have existed before intensive occupation began, c. AD 910.

The era of the Viking take-over of York clearly saw a revitalisation of the Coppergate area after centuries of abandonment, and the archaeological evidence demonstrates the initial stages of regeneration taking place. This, however, was only the start of urban renewal in Viking Age York—more innovations with further reaching implications were shortly to be introduced.

ABOVE
47 Complete late ninth-century cooking pot of York ware type. Height 15.5cm.

OPPOSITE
35 The Coppergate Anglian helmet, c. AD 750–75.

5
Viking Settlement - Planning and Prosperity

At some time *c.* AD 910 there was a fundamental change in the way the Coppergate area was used, a change which has had repercussions right down to the twentieth century and which even affected the recent redevelopment plans. The event in question was the laying out of new tenement boundaries in the form of post-and-withy fences and the erection of buildings at the modern Coppergate street frontage (48). This took place simultaneously over all four tenements within the excavated area and its date is calculated on the evidence of coins, themselves datable within approximately a decade, found below and above the new tenements. This happened either because an individual landlord decided to reorganise his property, or because of the corporate decision of a ruling body to encourage the expansion of the town and its economy and to provide what was to be, in effect, a combined industrial and residential estate on the edge of the contemporary settlement. This second alternative may sound far-fetched at so early a date, but there are historical grounds for suggesting that at this time York was ruled not by a king but by a council of

important citizens who can be seen exercising their collective power in the anonymous coinage issued in York *c.* 905–27, and who a little later, in the face of a bewildering series of regal comings and goings in the period *c.* 939–54, presumably provided the necessary continuity of leadership and stability which maintained the city's prosperity.

Whoever took the decision to establish the new tenements, they were laid out in plots of equal width, with boundaries close to the earlier divisions of the site but varying from their alignment by about ten degrees. It was these new boundaries which remained with a minimum of variation for the next one thousand years. Some were lost when properties were amalgamated in the late nineteenth century, and the demolition work and site clearance of 1976 accounted for another between the Craven's sweet factory and the White Horse public house, but even today the outer boundaries of the new Wimpey development almost directly overlie Viking Age boundaries laid out in *c.* 910.

This is a remarkable example of pre-Norman town planning, comparable to contemporary examples recently discovered at, for example, Lincoln and Dublin, and its implications for York are wide ranging. Although the tenth-century street frontage was found to be outside the limits of the excavation underneath the modern Coppergate, the street must surely have been laid out by this time. The only question is, was it created during the first decades of

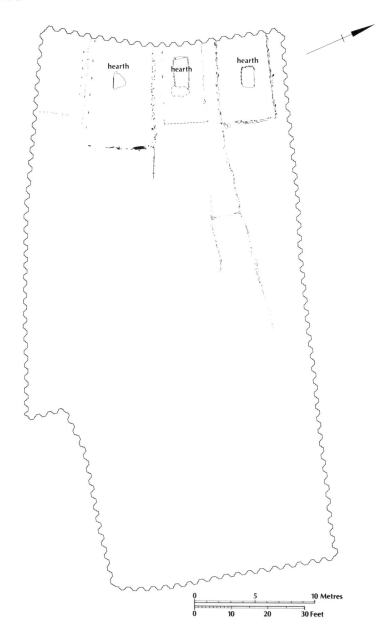

hearth

hearth

hearth

0   5   10 Metres

0   10   20   30 Feet

ABOVE
48 The Coppergate site in the period *c*. 910–970/80.

OPPOSITE
49 Excavating the floors of two early tenth-century wattle buildings, each with a central hearth: each white label marks a post or stake.

Scandinavian occupation when activity on the site was so much less intensive? This question will remain unanswered unless excavation below the modern street line takes place, an unlikely event. However, the vivid contrast between the types of layers deposited before and after this redevelopment of *c.* 910 suggests that there was some significant alteration of circumstances in the area which either encouraged or resulted from the intensive occupation and activity on the new tenements, and this alteration is most likely to have been the creation of what we know as Coppergate. This in turn was probably linked to a development of the river crossing on the site of the present Ouse Bridge, and although it is possible that there was only a ford there then, it seems likely that a wooden bridge would have been built at an early date, perhaps a part of this programme of urban development.

The new buildings at the Coppergate street frontage were made of posts with strong, flexible branches (withies) woven around them, and measured on average at least 6.8m in length by about 4.4m in width (49). The fronts of all the buildings had been cut off by the insertion of the sheet piling at the modern pavement line—the Viking Age buildings extended, inaccessible, below the present pavement. It seems that any available wood was used in their construction if it was the right size, although there was a preference for hazel and oak. These structures may sound flimsy, but if well built they would have had considerable flexible strength. They also sound draughty, but this problem may have been countered either by textile drapes, skins and hides hung on the insides of their walls, or by coating their outer sides with clay which hardened into daub, a waterproof coating. There is no firm evidence for the drapes theory, but literary sources tell that it was a feature of aristocratic households, and there is no reason why the practice should not have been copied in a humbler way lower down the social scale. The daub is more problematical—pieces were found during the excavation, with the impressions of withies and posts visible on one or occasionally both sides, but none was in position on a wall. Therefore it is possible that they were associated with internal fittings such as ovens and had nothing to do with walls. Perhaps a detailed consideration of all the impressions will allow us to diagnose their purpose, but at the moment we cannot tell.

Equally problematic are the roofs of these buildings—they may have been of thatch, or turf, or a mixture of both. At one time it was thought that they might have had wooden shingles, for several boards of the appropriate size and shape were found with peg-holes in them, but these were later identified as wooden spades, and so can be discounted. With no visible evidence to decide this turf and thatch question, the only hope of an answer lies with the scientists of the Environmental Archaeology Unit, who may be able to recognise in soil samples taken from within these buildings the remains of distinctive insect communities which characteristically live in one or other sort of roof.

50 Successive phases of tenth-century wattle buildings revealed in a vertical face of soil. Scale measures 1m.

The buildings' floors were simply of earth, with their level constantly rising as people carried in mud on the soles of their shoes, and by modern Western standards the buildings seem rather squalid, as all sorts of domestic rubbish and debris, including food bones, were left lying on the floors and were trampled into them. This slow raising of the floor level was paralleled outside by the accumulation of natural debris such as rotting vegetation and windblown and waterborne silts, coupled with the considerable quantities of domestic refuse generated by each tenement. Some of this was just dumped on the ground surface, and some was buried in rubbish pits or put down disused wells and cess pits, but however it was disposed of it helped to raise the level of the backyards.

This rise in level was accentuated by the fairly frequent need to repair or replace the wattle buildings. They were extremely vulnerable to fire, being set close together and constructed of readily inflammable materials, and if one caught fire a considerable number of adjacent buildings was also at risk. Charred upright posts and extensive layers of ash and charcoal testify to several fires which swept along this part of Coppergate and necessitated a complete rebuilding programme. Decay resulting from natural causes also required that walls and roofs, or at least parts of them, were repaired quite frequently. Because of the continual rise in ground level, which in the tenth century was building up at a rate averaging approximately 2cm per year, each rebuilding or phase of repair was at a slightly higher level than its predecessor, and it was therefore usually possible (although often difficult) to distinguish these separate periods in each building's life, even when its walls were rebuilt in the same position time after time (50).

Although the basic concept of walls constructed of wooden uprights with withies woven between remained current for over half a century, there were variations in the details of construction—for example whether posts, stakes or upright planks were used, at what spacings they occurred, and how they were held in place in the ground (51). These factors in turn may well have influenced the way the roof was constructed, and altered the appearance of the building; they may also represent a progression of ideas about building techniques, and so are well worth studying from that viewpoint. Another fascinating question is raised because it seems that similar changes in building practice took place simultaneously on each of the four tenements. Does this mean that all four were in the ownership of a single landlord, who controlled rebuilding and imposed a uniform approach across all his properties even though the work was done by the occupiers; or alternatively, is it because the rebuilding was in the hands of professional builders who had their own evolving techniques?

Although a reasonably clear picture of the buildings' external appearance should eventually be assembled, their internal arrangements are for the most part more difficult to conjure up, as the evidence is so meagre. The most obvious features within are substantial hearths, measuring up to 1.8m × 1.2m, positioned in the centre of the floor and replaced one above the other as the floor level rose (49, 52). They were usually made up of a clay base surrounded by a well-defined edge of limestone blocks or re-used Roman tiles, but on at least one occasion wooden beams form this edge. The hearths were so large and so carefully prepared because the occupants were trying to minimise the risk of fire by containing embers and sparks on this well-defined area—only small parts of each hearth were actually used for building fires, as the limited extent of burnt clay testifies.

Surprisingly, at least to the excavators, it seems that some quite substantial pits were dug *inside* the buildings while they were in use—pits measuring up to 2.4m × 2.2m. When found these were full of rubbish, but perhaps they were originally used for storing raw materials, valuables, or some other necessities; presumably they were originally covered by planks, but no sign of any survived.

The only possible indication of internal fittings came in the form of two lines of stakes, facing each other across one building, and running parallel to and 60cm inside the walls for approximately two thirds of the excavated length of the building, before

curving in to join the wall-line (52). These may be interpreted as forming the outer edges of two benches, made by filling the space between the stake lines and the walls with soil or turf—the stakes had withies woven between them to stop the infill from collapsing over the floor. The lack of furniture may initially suggest a rather spartan and uncomfortable existence, but doubtless there were stools, chairs, tables and other items of which no trace remained.

The large quantities of objects which were either lost or discarded on the earth floors of these buildings have allowed the tasks carried on inside some of them to be identified with certainty. The occupations of the inhabitants of the two southern tenements have not yet been recognised, but both of the tenements at the northern end of the site seem to have been occupied by metalworkers, who left a vast and varied amount of technological debris behind them. Although some of their work may have been carried out in the open air behind the buildings, they also used the large hearths for heating metals, as is shown by the many fragments of crucibles and other containers for molten metal which were found around them. The pottery crucibles were all small, and some were tiny, the same size and shape as a thimble (53 *a* and *b*). Minute spots of metal could still be seen on some, and it was important to recognise this quickly so that the pieces were not allowed to go through the normal cleaning process which would have dislodged the metal. These residues have been analysed in the Department of the Environment's Ancient Monuments Laboratory and traces of lead, copper alloy, silver and gold have been identified. As expected, gold was comparatively rare, but silver working was quite common. In addition, there is evidence for glass-making, particularly the production of glass with a high lead

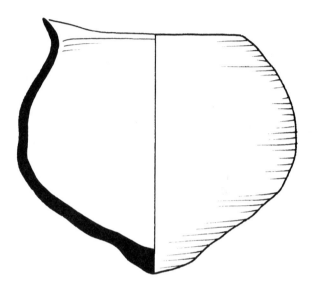

OPPOSITE
51 Tenth-century wattle wall supported by closely spaced external posts. Scale measures 20cm.

52 Tenth-century wattle building with central hearth and stake-revetted wall-benches at either side. Scale measures 1m.

ABOVE
53 *a* and *b* Pottery crucibles found in the early tenth-century workshops. Height (*a*) 6cm (*b*) 3.3cm.

content, and for iron working. The metalworkers were clearly not narrow specialists, but were masters of a range of techniques.

Other evidence supports some of these findings. For example, pieces of galena were found, a shiny, heavy ore which yields both lead and small amounts of silver, and so too were lumps of iron slag, solidified into the hemispherical shapes of the furnace bottoms where they formed. No metal-workers' tools have been positively identified yet—there are no easily recognisable smith's tongs, for instance—but some of the iron punches and other small tools which were found could have been used specifically by metalsmiths, and research into this possibility is still in progress.

Clues to some of the items which the smiths produced came in the form of stone or clay moulds into which molten metal was poured. The most common moulds are made of stone and are square in cross-section, with slots cut into each face (54). They were used for the casting of ingots, which were a convenient form in which to store metal before remelting it and making finished objects. Silver ingots or parts of them were sometimes used in everyday commercial dealings instead of or in addition to the silver penny coinage, but the only ingot fragment found at Coppergate was one made of copper alloy, and probably represents part of a metalworker's holding of his raw material. Only one mould, made from a Roman tile, had other shapes cut into it, and these have been provisionally identified as blanks for pins, brooches or pendants which would have been finished off and decorated by the craftsman after the basic shape had been cast in the mould (55).

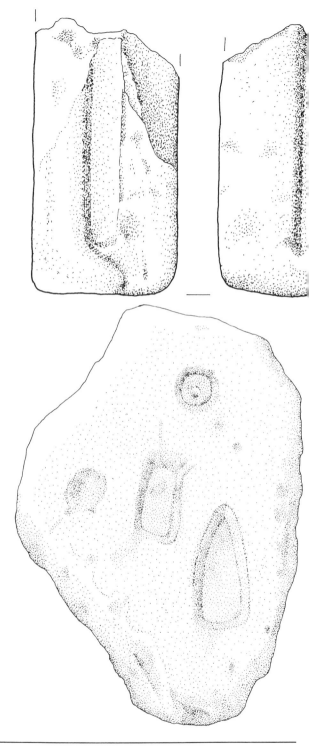

TOP
54 Four faces and cross-section of a fragmentary stone ingot mould. Length 7.7cm.

BOTTOM
55 Roman tile, re-used in the tenth century as a mould for casting metal-working blanks. Length 14.8cm.

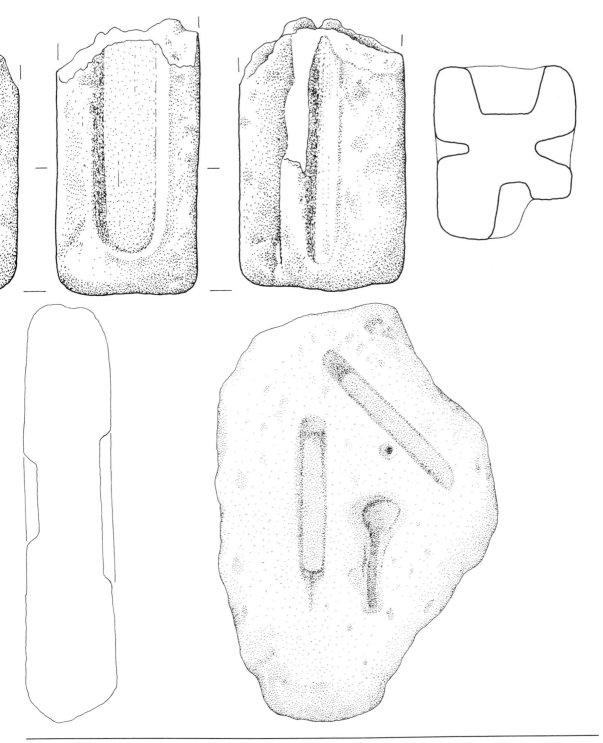

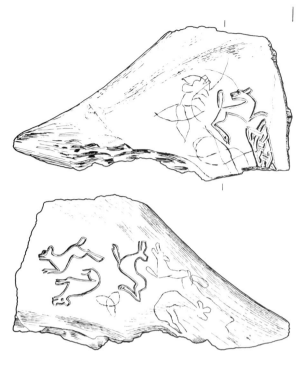

56 Tenth-century craftsman's bone trial-piece with animal and interlace motifs. Length 10cm.

57 *a* and *b* Fragment of a cow's rib, used as an artist's trial-piece in the tenth century. Length 18.2cm.

An idea of the sorts of decoration sometimes used can be gained from an examination of two pieces of animal bone which the craftsmen had used as convenient surfaces for practising their repertoire of designs. One has athletic dog-like animals cut into it (56); the other shows a more careful approach, with five successive attempts to construct an intricate piece of animal interlace (57 *a* and *b*). Once the pattern had been successfully mastered on the motif piece, then the craftsman could use it as a model for decorating whatever object he worked.

Only a few objects which were probably made in these workshops have been identified with certainty. One is a small disc of lead, decorated on one side with a meaningless imitation of an inscription in the angular runic lettering which was a common inheritance of both the English and Scandinavians at this time (58). It may have been intended as a brooch or pendant, but it had been lost or discarded after casting, before the finishing touches were applied. This accounts for the ragged, untrimmed edge to the disc, and the projection at one point of surplus metal marking the spot at which the molten lead was poured into the mould. The same unfinished appearance also singles out a bow brooch as a product of the workshops, and this is a particularly interesting specimen since it seems to be copied from a type common on the Continent (59).

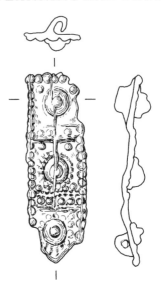

ABOVE
58 Unfinished lead-alloy pendant, tenth century,
decorated with a runic or pseudo-runic inscription.
Diameter 2cm.

RIGHT
59 Unfinished tenth-century bow brooch of lead alloy.
Length 5cm.

BELOW
60 Disc brooches from the Viking Age levels, made of
silver (*centre right*), silver plated lead alloy (*top left*),
copper alloy (*bottom row*) or lead alloy (*others*).

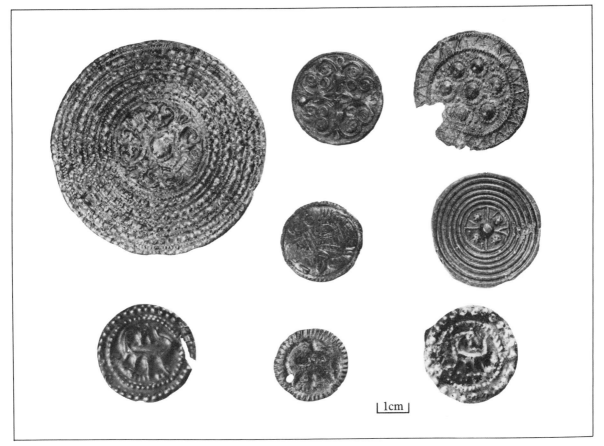

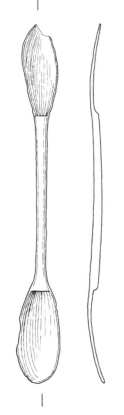

Other jewellery found in and around the buildings may also have been manufactured there. There is, for example, an unusual number of disc brooches, the majority made from a lead alloy which at a distance could be mistaken for silver (60). Among these is a badly made brooch, decorated with a stylised animal design which includes Scandinavian elements, but which is spoilt by being pock-marked with the small cavities called casting-bubbles which occur when molten metal is poured unevenly and too rapidly into a mould. Such a poor piece may be a reject, perhaps manufactured on site and unsaleable. Its interest lies partly in the fact that it is almost exactly identical to a brooch found in York nearly a century ago — it is a piece of cheap, tenth-century fashion jewellery, mass-produced for York's market (61). Indeed, many of the other brooches are clearly cheap lead alloy imitations copying more expensive originals which were hand-made and individually decorated in silver.

As well as down-market jewellery, the metalworkers may also have been making other items. Metal spoons, usually double-ended, and made from iron with a tin coating to give a silvery appearance, are quite rare in Viking Age England, but the Coppergate site yielded three from within and around the buildings, so they too may be a product of the workshops (62).

The metalworking remains described so far are more than sufficient to make these Coppergate workshops of great importance in the study of tenth-century technology. However, there is also evidence that the metalworkers had an even more interesting role in the community — that they acted as royal agents in the production of the silver pennies which were the principal currency in

TOP
61 Lead-alloy disc brooch of tenth-century date, decorated with a poorly executed Anglo-Scandinavian animal design and disfigured by casting bubbles. Diameter 2.75cm.

BOTTOM
62 Iron double-ended spoon, with tin coating. Tenth century. Length 10.6cm.

tenth-century England. This was first hinted at when a folded lead strip was discovered, bearing impressions that had been made when test-striking the two iron dies used to mint a penny of the English King Eadwig (955–59) (63). Later a second of these trial-pieces was found, this time for one die of a penny of the English King Athelstan (925–39) (64) and eventually a fragment of a third, again for Athelstan, came to light. Since there are only six similar objects from the whole of Anglo-Saxon England, this group pointed clearly to the existence of specialist coiners on the site.

The impressions on the first two trial-pieces were extremely crisp in all their details, and provided the answers to several basic and some more searching questions about how coins were produced in the early tenth century. For example, the outer limits of the impressions were circular, proving that the die-heads themselves were round, rather than square as some people had thought likely. Again, at ninety-degree intervals around the design's edge were small pimples which represent pinpricks into the die-head. Together with fine curving lines visible within the coin design, these are the marks made by compasses used to provide guide-lines for the die-engraver as he laid out the design. Details such as these are a revelation to coin experts and provide them with an unparalleled new range of information to think about.

Further, confirmatory evidence of an even more remarkable nature came with the discovery of an iron coin die, the first to be found anywhere in the Viking world (65). It was a totally unexpected find,

ABOVE
63 Lead trial-piece with test impressions of the two dies used to strike a coin of King Eadwig (955–59). The impression on the right is reversed because the die was engraved incorrectly. Length 15.3cm.

BELOW
64 Lead trial-piece with test impression of coin die of King Athelstan of York (927–39) with the inscription REGNALD MO EFORWI, 'Regnald the moneyer at York'. Average diameter 3cm.

because contemporary law codes spelt out in simple terms the penalties that would be inflicted for abusing the privileged position of being a royal moneyer, and failure to account for each and every coin die would certainly amount to abuse, for its possession amounted virtually to a 'licence to print money'. King Athelstan, for example, specified in his laws that 'if a moneyer is convicted, the hand with which he committed the crime is to be struck off, and put on the mint'. This sanction, presumably coupled with a normally vigorous administration, had left numismatists without any clear idea of what a die of this period looked like, or how it was made. The Coppergate die has therefore thrown totally new light on minting techniques.

It is cylindrical in shape, flaring outwards at its base, where a tang protruded which could be fixed into a bench or anvil. The tang has its end broken off, but otherwise the die is complete. The uppermost part of the shaft is slightly different in colour from the remainder, and seems to be specially or separately prepared. The reason for this is probably the need to have a specially hardened head, since it was this upper end of the die which received the full shock of the hammer-blow when a coin was struck. The face of the die is engraved with an abbreviated inscription in Latin (66). The engraving is deliberately retrograde, making the inscription appear to read backwards, so that when struck it will read correctly. The inscription can be translated as 'the money of St Peter', and it is generally believed that this wording is a reference to the cathedral church of York, which is dedicated to St Peter, although the church authorities were not responsible for governing the city or producing its currency. In contrast to this religiously inspired inscription, a sword and a hammer are also included in the design. The shape of the sword's handle suggests that it is modelled on a Viking weapon, and the hammer is the pagan emblem Mølnir, symbol of the Norse god Thor, the thunderer and god of war. If these identifications are correct, the die-head shows the two elements in York's Anglo-Scandinavian population represented symbolically on their joint coinage, one of the few tangible signs of a mutual acceptance which is more clearly witnessed in contemporary writings which still referred to 'the Northumbrians' rather than 'the Vikings' even at the height of Viking royal power. Coins with this design were issued c. 920–27, two generations after the Vikings first arrived at York.

Confirmation that die-heads were made separately came in the last weeks of the excavation with the discovery of a second die represented only by its head, which had become detached from the body (67). However, it was not necessarily this breakage which led to the die's loss, for the engraved face had itself partly disintegrated under the pressure of persistent hammering. Despite this, it is still clear that the die was used when the English King Athelstan was in control of York, 927–39.

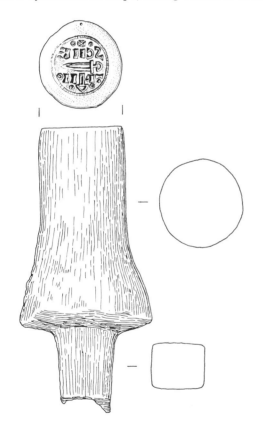

65 Iron coin die for early tenth-century St Peter's penny. Height 9.2cm.

The combined evidence of the metalworking debris, the three trial-pieces and the two coin dies leads inescapably to the conclusion that at Coppergate the only coin-mint known in the Viking world has been discovered. How did it come to be sited in a workshop in a thriving manufacturing quarter of York? The answer lies in the policy adopted by kings throughout western Europe at this time, in which minting places were established wherever there was economic justification. This meant in the towns and cities, and the prosperity and commercial importance of each town could be judged in relation to its neighbours and rivals by the number of moneyers whom the king appointed to control the minting. Each moneyer had his own coin dies, normally with his name engraved as part of the design on the reverse die, and he was responsible for their use, their security and for maintaining the standard weight and silver content of the coins struck from them. During the reign of Athelstan York is known to have had twelve moneyers, a number which emphasises its economic supremacy in the north of England and its national importance, since for most of the Viking Age it was outminted only by London. Now for the first time there is evidence for working conditions and techniques in one of the moneyers' workshops where the great wealth of England was turned into coin of the realm. Once minted, the coins could be transported over long distances as the result of trading, looting or extortion such as Danegeld payments handed over by the English to buy peace from Viking raiders. Indeed, a penny struck from the Coppergate Athelstan die has been recognised in the Danish national coin collection in Copenhagen, proof of Viking Age mobility around the North Sea (67).

TOP
66 Iron die-head for a St Peter's coin minted at York in the early tenth century. The head is deliberately engraved in reverse to give a correct impression. Diameter 2.8cm.

BOTTOM
67 Broken head of an iron coin die for King Athelstan of York (927–39) and a silver penny struck from the die. Diameter of die-head 3cm.

68 Cleaning a tenth-century wattle-lined pit.

Behind the buildings on the street frontage, the tenements ran back down the slope of the river terrace towards the River Foss. There were no other buildings here, but instead virtually the whole area was cut by a succession of holes which, when excavated, gave the site a cratered appearance. These holes had been dug originally for a variety of purposes. Some, lined with barrels, were probably wells; some, lined with woven withies, may have been used for storage (68); others served as latrines and cess pits. Whatever their original function, all were eventually filled up with domestic rubbish, and so were a rich source of interesting, though often broken, objects. They also held huge quantities of animal bones, oyster shells, and other less obvious food remains which are summarised on page 92ff.

The constant cycle of pit-digging, filling up and replacement meant that the soil of these backyards was regularly disturbed and the remains of old rubbish was brought to the surface. This goes some

way towards accounting for the large quantities of animal bones lying around on successive surfaces in the backyards. However, it is quite likely that some rubbish was discarded directly into the backyards without ever being buried, and the presence of fresh food debris helped to account for the presence of scavenging animals and birds whose own remains were also found.

The mixture of soft, rich organic soil and rubbish would have rapidly come to resemble a quagmire

OPPOSITE
42 Tile base of glass-making furnace, c. AD 860 (p. 43). Scale measures 50cm.

43 Glass fragments found near the ninth-century glass furnace (p. 44).

after a period of rain, when the sloping surface became treacherous and slippery—as the excavation team discovered only too easily. Surprisingly, remarkably little effort was put into lessening the risk of a fall, and serious attempts at providing and retaining a path were made only occasionally. On one tenement a horizontally-laid screen made from interwoven withies ran back from the rear of the buildings (69); when the rising ground level covered it over, it was replaced firstly with a stronger trackway made of cross-beams pegged into supporting wooden boughs (70), and this in turn was replaced again with a path of wattle. When this third pathway was covered, no further attempt was made to replace it, and the occupants must have relied on wariness alone, as their neighbours had apparently done all along.

44 The misleading 'glazed' appearance on the outside of pottery found near the ninth-century glass furnace (p. 44).

45 Glass deposits on the inside of pottery found near the ninth-century glass furnace (p. 44).

69 A wattlework pathway leading to a tenth-century building out of the picture on the right. The path has been cut away in the foreground by a later semi-basement building, and is bounded on its far side by a wattle fence forming a property boundary. Scale measures 1m.

The raider/trader who had been brought up in York in the decades before AD 900, and then travelled the Viking world to seek his fortune, would hardly have recognised the Coppergate area if he had made a return visit c. 930, when an English king was temporarily back in control. Coppergate was now a busy street lined with closely packed timber buildings, their eaves so close that they almost touched. On their frontages stalls sold all manner of domestic essentials and luxuries, and business was brisk, for Coppergate was one of the main cross-town arteries. The sounds and smells of workshops making leather and metal items were particularly noticeable, but in the backyards behind the buildings the raw materials and manufacturing debris were mixed with the remains of domestic rubbish, for these buildings were both houses and workshops. Down by the river cargo vessels and rowing boats were drawn up, the cargo ships disgorging their cargoes of foreign luxuries, German wine and raw materials such as Baltic amber. The area was served by several churches—in Coppergate there was All Saints', and just around the corner was St Mary's, both of which had their graveyards around them. The overall picture was one of prosperity—no matter whether a Viking or an Anglo-Saxon was king, it was business as usual at York's commercial heart. Even a bewildering succession of short-lived rulers in the period 939–54 apparently did not affect the city's booming economy, and the expulsion of the last Viking king, Erik Bloodaxe, in 954 also seems not to have caused any noticeable commercial disruption. As the tenth century drew towards its close, with English rulers acknowledged as kings in York, the only change recognisable in Coppergate was in the homes and workshops of the occupants.

70 Plank pathway made of cross-beams, mostly removed in the tenth century, pegged into axial beams (that on the left obscured by later wattlework). Scale measures 50cm.

6
The Later Viking Age - Continuity and Change

In the last two or three decades of the tenth century the thoroughly integrated Anglo-Scandinavian population of York was thriving—within England only London was a larger and wealthier city. At the very end of the century there may have been speculation that a Danish king might eventually supplant the nominal English authority in York, as Svein Forkbeard's raids on England gained momentum, but in general life was much as it had been for several generations.

There was, however, at this time a radical change in the appearance of the buildings at the Coppergate frontage. On all four tenements the wattle-walled houses-cum-workshops were rebuilt in a completely new style in which a semi-basement as much as 1.5m deep replaced a floor at ground level, and at least the lower 1.8m of the walls was fashioned from substantial oak planks and posts (71). Although these semi-basements may seem a peculiar type of building, the nature of the floor deposits indicates clearly that they were lived in, and were not just cellars for storage. On two of the tenements there were now two ranks of buildings, one at the street frontage and the other a few metres behind; on the third tenement there was only a single building at the frontage, and on the fourth a single structure of greater length, divided into two by a partition wall, replaced an earlier arrangement of separate buildings (72). The distribution patterns of different types of objects found in and around them

suggest that on the tenements with two separate buildings the front one served as living quarters (probably with a stall for selling goods on the street frontage) and the rear one functioned as a workshop. Because their front gables extended beyond the excavation's perimeter piling or because their rear walls had been destroyed by later disturbances, complete dimensions could be recovered in only two instances, both of them buildings in the rear rank. These measured 7.5–7.6m × 3.8–4m, but it does not follow that the street frontage buildings were identical in length, and as main living quarters they may have been rather longer. This type of building seems to have been first constructed at Coppergate in the period *c.* 970–80, when they appeared on several different tenements, again suggesting that, as with the post and withy buildings at the start of the century, there was a simultaneous reconstruction across the four excavated tenements. Although these buildings remained popular sufficiently long for some to require replacing in the early decades of the eleventh century, there was no recurrence of the type later in the site's history.

The quite precise dates quoted above are available thanks to the dating method called dendrochronology, or tree-ring dating. Its theory is simple—for every year of a tree's life a single growth ring is formed, the size of which varies according to the climatic conditions that year. Within a particular climatic zone, all the growth rings of a particular

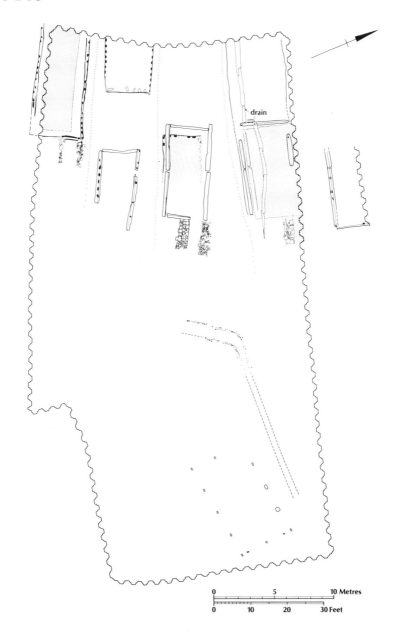

drain

| 0 | | 5 | | 10 Metres |
| 0 | 10 | 20 | | 30 Feet |

72 The Coppergate site during the later Viking Age, *c.* 970/80–*c.* 1060. Stippling indicates buildings of this phase replaced during the period. The drain in the northern tenement belongs with the later building there. Features beyond the inner shoring are those recorded during the watching brief.

species will be the same size relative to previous years, thus forming a uniform pattern of rings. This fact is the basis of dendrochronology, which in Britain is normally based on a study of oak timber, since oak was most frequently used in ancient buildings for the main structural elements. A reference master pattern can be made by measuring the annual variations of the growth rings, starting with a tree felled at the present day and then extending back into the past by overlapping with timbers from increasingly old buildings—medieval churches are a particularly good source of material. Excavated timbers can then be added to the pattern, and it can be used to date any suitably large timber with sufficient growth rings (usually at least fifty) to ensure that its pattern can be slotted into the known,

dated pattern with confidence, and without the possibility that the match between excavated timbers and master pattern is coincidental. At best, dendrochronology may pinpoint the precise year when a building was erected, and at least is likely to provide an estimate to within a few decades, always provided that the timber in question was newly felled and not re-used.

To erect a building of the semi-basement type, a rectangular hole of appropriate size was first dug out to a depth of about 1.5m, with deeper channels along the edges of the cut where the walls would be

73 The cut for a tenth-century sunken building, with foundation beams in place. Scale measures 2m.

bedded in. Sometimes massive horizontal oak beams (73) up to 7m long and 25cm × 8cm in cross-section provided a base for the wall-posts which were held in position behind a raised lip on the inner edges of the beams (74); sometimes the posts were set directly into the channel, resting on wooden pads for a little extra stability and as a slight protection against rotting. These posts, carefully squared and regularly spaced at short intervals, supported layers of horizontal oak planks which were laid edge upon edge, and these in turn prevented the earth behind from cascading into the building (75). The upright posts seem to have been paired across the building's width, and were presumably held upright at their tops by beams spanning the building.

In all of the construction described so far there was not a nail, a peg or a joint, and the structure stood by pressure of one timber on another. However, without the soil bank behind the horizontal planks they would have collapsed outwards like a pack of cards, so clearly above ground level there must have been a change in the method of building. Unfortunately there is only one clue to what happened at this level. At the very top of the tallest surviving upright posts, 1.75m above their base, they have been cut back to make a ledge or seating which could have supported another timber, and just below this seating a circular hole has been pierced through the centre of each post (76). What does this indicate? Perhaps that at this height there was a horizontal beam jointed into each of the

OPPOSITE
74 The lipped foundation beam for a tenth-century sunken building bearing the stub of an upright supporting horizontal planks behind. Scale measures 20cm.

ABOVE
75 The side wall of a tenth-century sunken building. Scale measures 1m.

uprights to provide lateral stability. But even if this was so, the appearance of the buildings from this point upwards is still highly conjectural and there is even some uncertainty about whether or not there was an upper storey. To restore the buildings with an upper storey would seem to pose problems over the stability of the lower timbers, but if there was no upper storey, and the buildings' roofs rested directly above the horizontal beam, then they would have protruded only a few metres above the ground surface. Although there would have been sufficient headroom inside, this reconstruction paints a picture of such a low-rise roofscape and a semi-

troglodytic existence for the occupants that it inspires disbelief in modern minds. Nevertheless, this latter suggestion seems easier to accept on the basis of the excavated evidence, and even much later, in the seventeenth century, sunken buildings of very similar type are known to have been constructed by colonists in New Amsterdam (now New York), New England and Virginia.

While all these buildings were essentially identical, some showed refinements on the basic design. Only one had remnants of a planked floor surviving, comprising joists which supported planks carefully cut to fit flush around the internal upright posts and to lap against the wall (77). A second building had cavity walls, made up of an inner and outer skin of horizontal planks with squared uprights between them, and additional uprights supporting the inner skin from within the building (78). This structure also had pairs of posts up its centre, the two posts of each pair spaced about 1.3m apart and dividing the floor area into three narrow units. These posts, although rather insubstantial, may have acted as

ABOVE
76 Semi-collapsed wall of a tenth-century sunken building, showing seatings and dowel holes 1.75m from the base of the (originally) upright posts. Scale measures 50cm.

OPPOSITE
77 One corner of a tenth-century sunken building, showing floor joists and charred floor planks. Scale measures 20cm.

78 Excavating the 'cavity wall' tenth-century sunken building.

additional roof supports, but they are not paralleled in any of the other buildings. There was also a mat of fine twigs and brushwood all over its interior, a feature it shared with a building on the adjacent tenement. There the willow twigs were interlinked in one corner, proving that they were not simply rubbish thrown into the building but were an integral part of its construction (79). Their function is uncertain but it is most likely that they acted as insulation, either woven together and attached somehow to the walls as screens, or put into the roof space.

For a long time one of the most puzzling questions about these buildings was the very obvious one: how did the occupants get in and out of them if they were sunk over 1.5m into the ground? Did they clamber up and down ladders, or was there some other method of entry? There were no clear signs of doorways in the long sides of any building, and it

79 Willow twigs, perhaps originally a form of insulation, inter-linked against the corner post in one of the sunken buildings. Scale measures 10cm.

seemed most likely that entrances would have been in the gable-ends. Unfortunately many of these had been destroyed by modern foundations, or were out of sight beyond the street-front piling. Where the gable-ends did survive they were sometimes continuous, with no sign of a door, but in one possible and two certain cases there were gaps in the back wall at one corner where the foundation beam was interrupted, and these seemed to indicate the position of doors. Yet if this was a correct interpretation each door would have opened against a vertical bank of earth unless there was an entrance-way dug into the soil behind, and any sunken entrance would soon have been filled up by

80 Stone-revetted entrance passage leading to a tenth-century sunken building already excavated at bottom of picture. Scale measures 50cm.

collapsing soil unless its sides were supported somehow. This problem was solved when eventually it was realised that what had at first been interpreted as the very disturbed remains of a stone-walled building immediately behind the door-gap of one of the workshops, was in fact the remains of two parallel walls which had lined the sides of a cutting which led to the doorway (80). The doorway and passageway had not been equated initially

82 Products of a woodturner's workshop—a cup, bowls, and waste turning cores. Diameter of largest bowl, 15.5cm.

because there was a six month gap between the dismantling of the building and the exposure of its entrance passage. Beyond the back door of the cavity-wall building there were slight remains of another similar arrangement (**71**, p. 80), and one side of a probable third was found in the last weeks of the excavation against the steel piling which had cut away its other side. Here again is an indication that these peculiar structures really were lived in at the subterranean level, and were not merely storage cellars below ground level buildings.

Some of the workshops were identifiable through the sort of debris embedded in their earth floors. The most easily recognised was one which had been inhabited by jewellers who used amber, the golden-yellow fossilised wood-resin, as their main raw material. They also had a side-line in objects made from jet, the soft, easily carved rock available at several places throughout northern Yorkshire, notably near Whitby. The amber was mostly turned into beads and pendants, and the jet into finger rings (**81**, p. 80). Waste pieces of both, and the discarded remains of items broken during their manufacture, were common discoveries here.

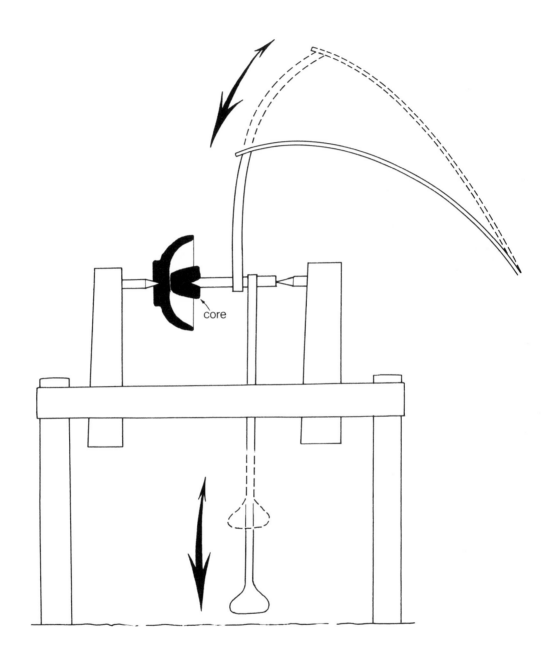

core

83 Reconstruction of how a pole-lathe was used by woodturners.

In the workshop next door there was evidence for a different industry, the making of wooden bowls and cups. Several partially broken or unfinished bowls were found as well as a few cups (82). There was also a large number of characteristically-shaped cores, looking like cut-down spinning-tops, which are produced during the turning process on a lathe, when a block of wood is gouged out until only the core remains at its centre (83). Many types of wood were used to make these bowls and cups, with ash, yew and maple probably the most common. Since people at this time did not use pottery plates, bowls or cups but generally took their food and drink from wooden vessels, lathe-turners provided much of the table-ware used in York, and there were probably several workshops there like this one at Coppergate.

This workshop may have given Coppergate its name, which place-name experts trace back to two words in Old Norse, the common language of Scandinavia in the Viking Age. It was also spoken by the Scandinavian settlers in York and became blended with the northern dialect of Old English spoken by the Anglo-Saxon inhabitants. The *gate* ending of Coppergate, found in so many street names in York and northern England, comes from Old Norse *gata*, meaning 'a street'—it is still to be found on name-plates for streets throughout Scandinavia. The 'Copper' part of Coppergate is a little more tricky to interpret, and several experts have thought that it relates to the metal copper, and have therefore suggested that Coppergate was 'the street of the copper-workers'. However, the most recent and authoritative study suggests that it derives from an Old Norse word *coppr*, 'a cup', and that the street was called 'cup-makers' street'. If the name was indeed given at the period to which these finds relate, it is clear from the jewellers' debris that in 'cup-makers' street' not all the tenements were occupied by cup-makers, but what crafts and trades were practised in the other two tenements remains something of a mystery, since there was no obvious concentration of tell-tale debris to provide a clue.

Although the buildings had been changed in design and appearance, the backyards continued to be used as they had been earlier—wells, rubbish pits, storage pits, cess pits and latrines were all dug into the slope. At the river-ward end of one property a new building was erected *c.* AD 1030 (72). Measuring 8.4m by 4.6m, its only remains were the rather decayed stumps of some of the main wall posts or, when even these did not survive, stains in the soil marking their original position (84). This poor state of preservation was due largely to the fact that at this point, nearer the river, there was hardly any build-up of the organic-rich debris which cocooned the building remains at the street frontage and thus preserved them—these deposits gradually thinned out down the slope towards the river, where they were increasingly distant from the main focus of occupation and activity which generated this debris.

On the basis of the excavated evidence there is no indication of the use to which this building was put, for there was no trace of recognisable floor deposits and no group of characteristic objects to pin down a specific activity carried on here, but its position suggests that it may have served as a store-house for goods unloaded from ships at the river's edge, or even perhaps as a boat-shed, although the water's edge was probably fifty metres or more away, beyond the excavated area. What lay within this fifty metres is unknown.

This building would have been vulnerable to rain-water sheeting down the slope in bad weather, and in order to protect it from this hazard a shallow, curving storm-water gulley was dug beyond its upper end to channel water around it. This gulley was lined with wattlework to prevent its sides from collapsing, but it still had to be replaced at least once as it became clogged with debris.

Bearing in mind the manufacturing that was in progress in the street frontage workshops, it is tempting to speculate that raw materials might have been brought to York by ship, offloaded at the Foss edge, stored in the nearby building until required, and then carried up the slope to the workshop area, whence, as finished products, the manufactured goods were moved to stalls on the street frontage for sale. This picture may be correct, but if this was how the occupants of this one tenement organised their

84 Foundations of an early eleventh-century building, perhaps a warehouse. Scale measures 2m.

supply and storage of raw materials, their neighbours did not copy their example, for no other tenements seem to have had buildings in a similar position near the waterside.

The property owner in Coppergate who invested in his new building *c.* 1030 was presumably confident that York's Anglo-Scandinavian prosperity and way of life would continue into the foreseeable future. The prospects of eventual conquest by the Norman French was undreamt of; but within a generation the undreamt of had happened and the hey-day of Jorvik came to an end.

OPPOSITE
71 The rear rank of semi-basement buildings seen from above. Workshops are clearly visible in the central two tenements (one cut by a nineteenth-century well), two foundation beams from the rear room of a two-roomed structure form a right angle on the tenement to the left, and the stone outline of an entrance passage into a building not yet excavated can be seen on the tenement to right. Scales measure 2m (p. 67).

81 Amber and jet found in and around one of the tenth-century workshops (pp. 76, 87).

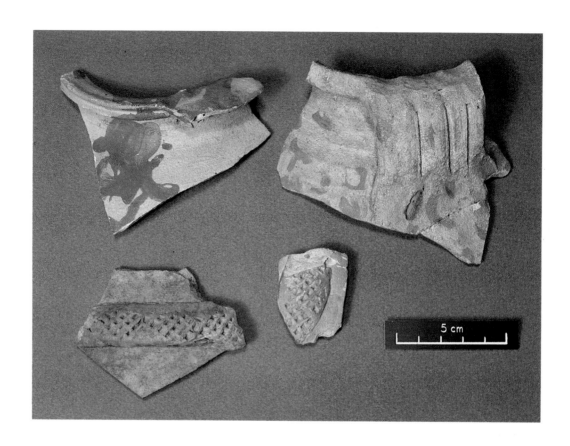

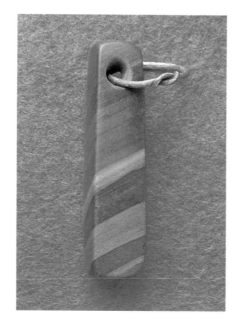

7
Everyday Life in Jorvik

The discovery of the incredibly well-preserved sequence of tenth-century buildings was one of the most important results of the excavation, but equally exciting and informative was the wide range of objects found in and around them. Several thousand items of all sorts were recovered, some broken but many intact, and most in a remarkably good state of preservation, whether they were made of stone, metal or glass, wood, leather or textile. Together they form what is probably the most comprehensive selection of personal possessions and domestic paraphernalia of this period ever found in Britain, and they throw light on a wide variety of aspects of everyday life in the heart of a flourishing urban community.

The wealth which their manufacturing activities earned for them enabled the craftsmen of Coppergate to live in some style, and to buy non-essential items made by other specialists in the city. Just a few examples from several hundred will illustrate this point. Bone and antler were important raw materials at this time, being used to make simple items such as pins, needles, combs and knife-handles, which today would often be made from plastics or metal. Many of the simpler types of bone and antler items were probably home-made—it did not take much practice to fashion a reasonable needle from a chicken's leg bone. But some other pieces, like the fine strap-end shown here (85), were almost certainly the products of professionals who were expert at carving intricate designs into small spaces—this piece measures only 6cm in length. Wood was perhaps the most widely used of all raw materials, and it too was made into elaborate items which were useful but which also displayed the wealth of the owner. As today, this applied in the field of

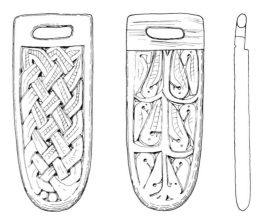

OPPOSITE
92 Red-painted and Badorf pottery, imported from the Continent (p. 87).

99 A tenth-century sharpening stone of banded slate (p. 91). Length 4.8cm.

ABOVE
85 Tenth-century bone strap-end. Length 6.2cm.

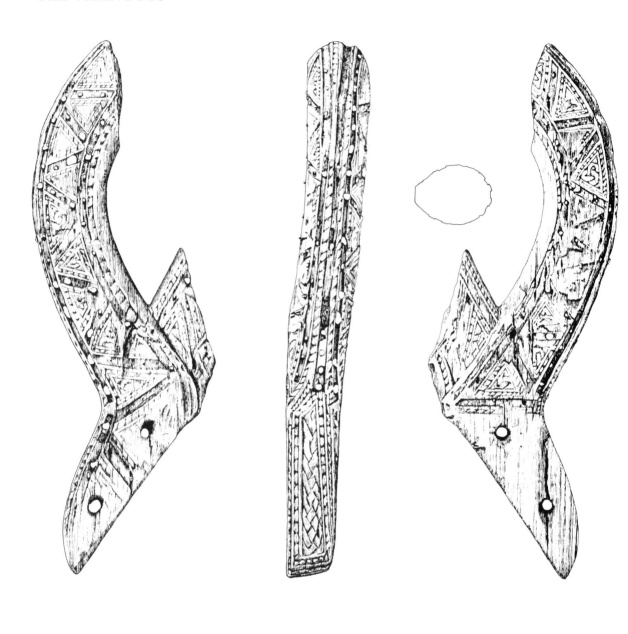

86 Fragmentary wooden saddle-bow. Tenth century.
Height 17.7cm.

87 Tenth-century leather shoes after conservation.

transport—the most elaborate piece of Viking Age wood-carving from England was found at Coppergate, in the form of one half of a highly ornate saddle-bow (86). It was made from oak, and was decorated all over with carved designs, mostly three-lobed knots in triangular panels, which had originally been highlighted with an inlay of horn held in place by silvery-looking nails. Close examination reveals that the carving is rather second-rate and careless in places, but even so the object still indicates what the wood-workers of York were capable of making.

Leather is another raw material which, like wood, is usually under-represented in the archaeological record. Several hundred leather items were found at Coppergate, of which the great majority were parts of shoes. The Viking Age citizens followed the normal practice at this time of having shoes and boots that had a single-piece flat sole, without a heel, which was sewn on to the upper part of the shoe. When the sole was worn it was taken off, thrown away and replaced—that is why worn soles are quite commonly found, and complete shoes are much rarer. Nonetheless, a wide range of shoe types and sizes was discovered (87). As well as shoes, a variety of other goods were made from leather, and among these were sword and knife scabbards. Some had elaborate designs stamped on to them, for instance the one shown here (88) and these, like the shoes, were probably made by professional leather-workers.

The items listed so far have shown that there was sufficient surplus cash in the craftsmen's pockets to allow them to live with a certain degree of style, rather than merely to survive on the bread-line, and when they died their final resting place in one of the

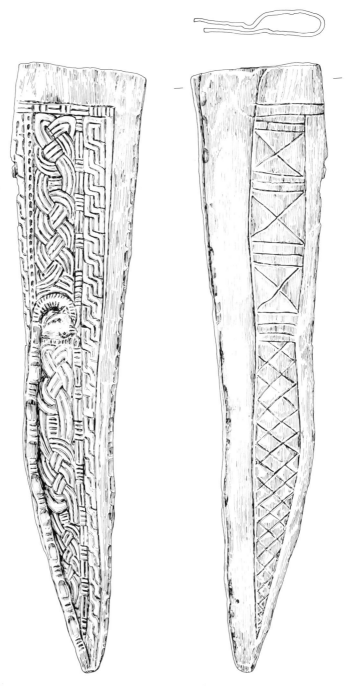

88 Decorated leather knife sheath. Tenth century.
Length 34.5cm.

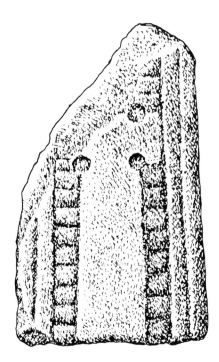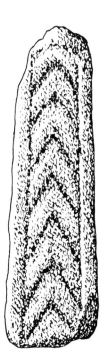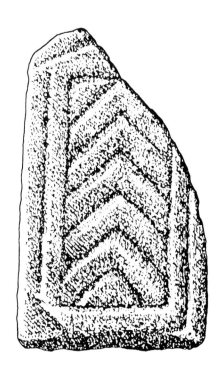

89 Fragmentary tenth-century gritstone grave-marker. Height 31.2cm.

city's churchyards could also be marked with a stylish stone memorial. Perhaps because the excavation was directly opposite the church of All Saints and its surrounding graveyard, and because another contemporary church, St Mary's, backed on to the site, parts of at least three decorated gravemarkers were recovered. One was designed to stand upright, with a cross carved on one side and a chevron design on the other (89). A second was just the corner from a carved slab, designed to lie over a grave, and decorated on its two edges with interlaced animal ornament in an English version of a Scandinavian style (90). The third was an even smaller fragment of a similar monument (91). When complete they would have been painted over in bright colours to highlight the decoration. These monuments, fashioned by masons who churned them out to fairly standardised patterns, must nevertheless have been quite expensive, and like the leather, wood and bone objects mentioned above, and the imported luxuries described below, they reflect the prosperity of York's craftsmen and merchants.

As well as goods made locally, or at least within north-eastern England, a relatively small number of objects which can be recognised as imported were also found in the Viking Age levels. They are among the most exciting discoveries, for they originated in widely spread areas of Europe and the East, but they are also among the most difficult to interpret, for they could have arrived at York for several different reasons. Some may have been objects of trade, deliberately brought from afar as luxury items and offered for sale in the market places of York, where not only the prosperous townsfolk but also the wealthy landowners and farmers from the surrounding countryside (or their agents) came to purchase the finer and more expensive things of life. International trading was certainly carried on in Jorvik—an English writer of *c.* AD 1000 could report that the city was 'filled with treasures of

90 Tenth-century limestone grave-cover fragment, its side decorated with an Anglo-Scandinavian interlaced animal design. Height 22.3cm.

merchants from many lands, particularly the Danes', and although it is not certain whether the Danes in question came from Denmark, or were immigrants already settled in England or other Scandinavian colonies in the west, the cosmopolitan character of York's commercial contacts is not in

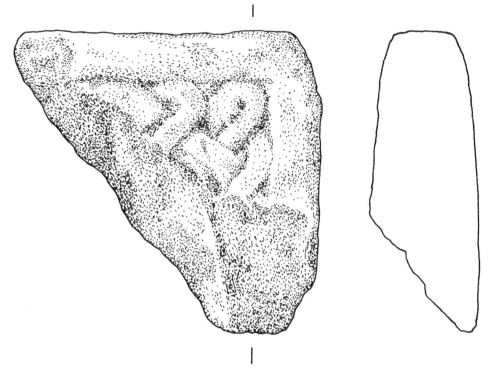

91 Fragmentary gritstone grave-cover with interlace decoration. Tenth century. Length 8cm.

doubt. English writers at this time habitually called Vikings or Scandinavians 'Danes', but the Scandinavians resident in York were probably of both Danish and Norwegian descent.

Among the goods which were probably brought to York in commercial quantities for sale was wine from the Rhineland. The wine itself is not preserved, of course, and the clue that it was brought comes in the form of a few pieces of pottery of distinctive types, manufactured in the Rhineland, which are the fragmentary remains of the large vessels in which it was transported (92, 93). German quern-stones made out of lava from the Niedermendig area were also imported on a commercial basis, as they had been centuries earlier in the Roman period. The texture of lava makes it particularly effective in grinding grain for bread, and in deference to both their teeth and their stomachs the citizens of York and their country cousins were sometimes prepared to pay the higher costs of these German products in preference to the cheaper local equivalents usually fashioned from gritstone, which were more likely to leave a gritty residue in the flour. Niedermendig querns would have formed a useful ballast for ships sailing to England from Germany or Holland, and this may also be true of the small sharpening stones made from Norwegian schist which were also found in fairly large numbers. Since it is likely that virtually every adult male always carried a knife with him (for domestic rather than defensive or aggressive use), whetstones were much in demand. Most are small enough to be carried around without inconvenience, and many retain the bored holes or nicked edges which show that they were originally suspended on a thong from the belt (94 a and b).

Other goods of Scandinavian origin which may indicate commercial contacts include the amber which was the principal raw material used in one of the late tenth-century jewellery workshops. It is possible that some of it was collected on the beaches of eastern England, carried there by tides and currents from the Baltic Sea where it is found in considerable quantities, but the large amount used in the Coppergate workshop is unlikely to have been acquired solely from within England, and most if not all was probably brought from Denmark. The few bowls of the soft and easily carved rock known as soapstone or steatite which were found on the site may, like the whetstones, have come from Norway; although soapstone was also available on the Shetland Islands, where Viking Age quarries have been found at Cuningsburgh, bowls from there do not normally have the iron handle that is still attached to one of the Coppergate fragments (95). These large bowls were particularly useful for cooking, having a greater capacity than the normal cooking pots.

Commercial links with more distant shores are shown in several items made from silk. These include a tiny double envelope of silk with a cross embroidered on its front (96). This feature suggests that the pouch originally contained a precious holy relic, perhaps represented by a few strands of linen found inside it. At this time the nearest production centre for silk was the Byzantine Empire on the north-east shores of the Mediterranean Sea, and this is the most likely place of origin for the pieces found at Coppergate, although a source even further away in the Middle East or China cannot be completely ruled out. The mechanics of the English end of this trade have been made a little clearer by the study of a silk cap which was retrieved from a contractors' excavation at 5–7 Coppergate, only fifty metres from the Viking Dig. Remarkably, the silk from which the cap was made shares an unusual weaving fault with silk found during excavations in Lincoln and this suggests strongly that both items were made from lengths of cloth cut from a single bale which had been offered for sale in both cities. This discovery links the two most important commercial centres in the Danelaw, the area of eastern England where Scandinavian settlement was commonest, and places them at one end of a trading network which was at least two thousand miles long.

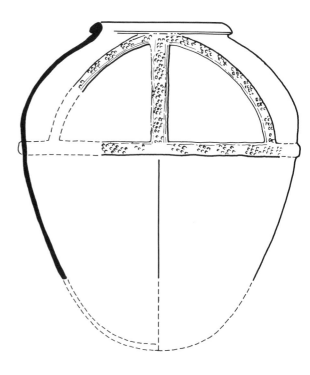

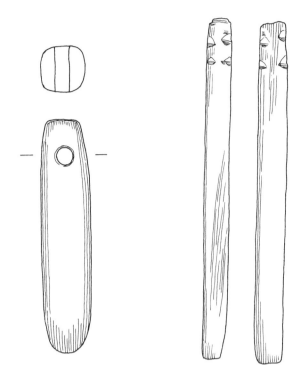

5cm

TOP LEFT
93 Reconstruction of a Badorf ware wine pitcher from the Rhineland. Height 36cm.

TOP RIGHT
94 Hone stones of tenth-century date, pierced or nicked for suspension. Lengths (*a*) 6.5cm (*b*) 9.5cm.

BOTTOM
95 The rim of a tenth-century soapstone bowl, pierced by an iron hoop for suspension.

Byzantium was not the limit of Viking Age York's commercial links. Within one of the early tenth-century buildings was found a seashell of an exotic form, the cowrie *Cypraea pantherina* (Solander) (97). This is a species which lives only in the waters of the Red Sea and the Gulf of Aden, and it must have been brought to York from one or other of those places. It probably had no commercial value, unless as an amulet or charm, and may be simply a traveller's souvenir or curio. Its archaeological importance is that it demonstrates contact between York and the Near East, and raises the possibility that other perishable, exotic goods may have changed hands in York. Oils, spices and perfumes would all leave no trace (except, perhaps, their containers), and slaves too may have been brought from the Orient.

York's links extended even further to the east, as is shown by a coin which bears an Arabic inscription recording that it was minted for the Arab caliph Isma'il Ibn Achmad at Samarkand in the early years of the tenth century (98). The fact that the coin is a contemporary forgery, made from a copper core covered with tin to imitate the genuine article of pure silver, does not alter the likelihood that it did originate at Samarkand, a town which stands at the western edge of the Himalayas, over three thousand miles from York. Although it probably came to York via Scandinavia, where tens of thousands of Arab coins have been found, it is still a pointer to the far-flung links which York enjoyed, however round-about the route.

Many other foreign objects were found in the Coppergate excavation, but they could be explained as the personal possessions of travellers, or as gifts

96 Silk reliquary pouch with embroidered cross,
tenth century. Height 3cm.

1cm

97 Cowrie shell from the Red Sea/Gulf of Aden, found in tenth-century levels.

from visitors, rather than as goods brought to York in quantity for sale. This category mainly includes jewellery—brooches from Germany, the Low Countries and Scotland, and dress pins from Ireland (p. 104). There are also the unusual objects which stood out from the run of locally made goods, but which are well-known from sites excavated abroad and are thus probably of foreign manufacture. Among these are a colourful whetstone of banded slate, similar to those found in some of the Viking Age graves in the eastern Swedish trading centre of Birka (99), and a decorated wooden box (100), its ash sides sewn together and pegged to an oak base-plate, which is paralleled at another Viking Age trading centre, Hedeby, near Schleswig, at the base of the Jutland peninsula, and formerly at the southern limit of Denmark.

In summary, imported objects reached York from Scandinavia, the Scandinavian colonies in Scotland and Ireland, continental Europe, the Byzantine Empire and the Near and Middle East (101). The city was a cosmopolitan mercantile centre, a market-place which provided expensive and luxury goods to a wide hinterland. The commercial enterprise and acumen of York's Anglo-Scandinavian merchants and traders is not in doubt, and their activities probably generated import levies for the city's rulers as well as lining the pockets of those involved. But the importance of foreign trade and contact should not be over-emphasised. Altogether, even counting every flake of amber waste and every piece of schist whetstone individually, these imported objects probably number less than five hundred of the fifteen thousand items found at Coppergate, and it is easy to overestimate their importance to the townsfolk of York, whose lifestyle would not have been noticeably affected if this outside contact had ceased. York's geographical position ensured that foreign contacts were relatively easy to maintain, but the city's international trade added to rather than accounted for its political and economic importance in northern England.

Having looked at some of the more unusual objects, it must be said that the most important result of the excavation is that it has shown what were the common things of everyday life in the Viking Age city. Throughout the tenth century the four excavated tenements (like those all around,

91

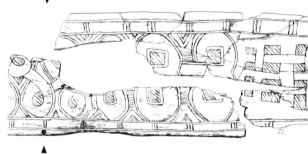

ABOVE
98 Contemporary forgery of a tenth-century Islamic silver coin from Samarkand, made of lead and tin on a copper alloy base.

OPPOSITE
100 The side of a circular box made of ash wood, tenth century, unrolled to show its decoration. Box diameter 19.6cm.

presumably) were not simply the sites where crafts and industries were carried out, but were homes for families who carried on their entire daily routine within and immediately around the small, closely-spaced wooden buildings. Here, for example, the mistress of the house prepared the family's meals. Quernstones show that she ground her own grain to make bread, and the thousands of pieces of broken cooking pots show us the standard form of kitchenware at this time (102). Other domestic pottery took the form of storage jars, bowls and jugs (103). Fortunately, we can pursue the question of diet and its effect upon health much further than merely looking at kitchen equipment, for recent advances in the study of environmental archaeology, particularly in the recovery of small and microscopic

remains during excavation and in their later interpretation, have allowed the Environmental Archaeology Unit at York University to study these topics in unparalleled detail.

The most obvious food remains are the bones of the big domesticated animals—cattle, sheep, goats and pigs. These must have been driven into York from the surrounding countryside and were sometimes, if not always, sold on the hoof and then butchered by the purchaser in his backyard. This is known because the bones include skulls with the marks of the violent blows which killed the animals—such bones would normally be found where butchery took place, and probably not anywhere else.

Rivers and the sea provided a large part of the

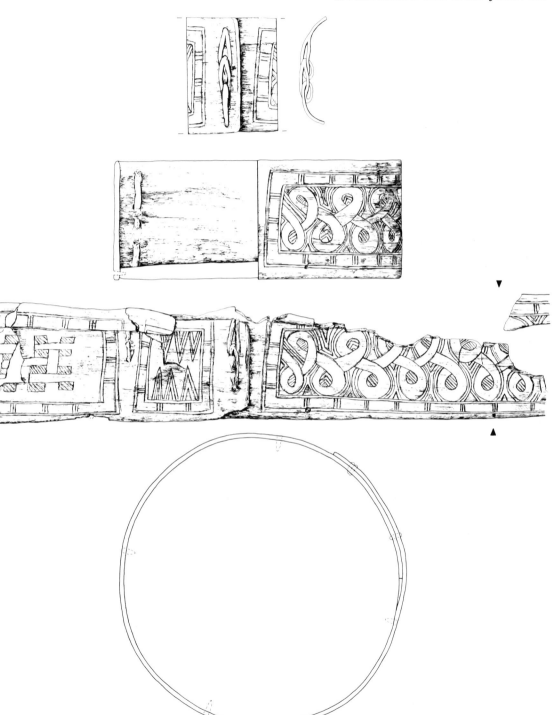

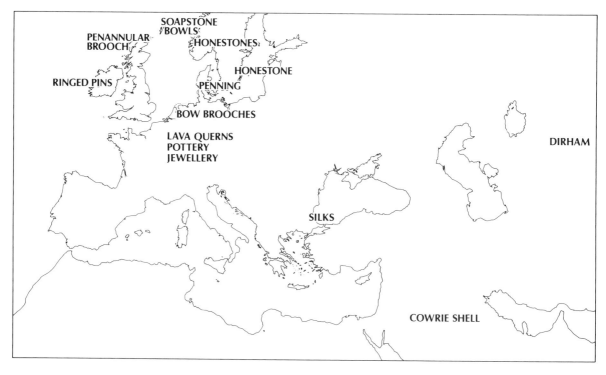

SOAPSTONE
BOWLS
PENANNULAR
BROOCH
HONESTONES
HONESTONE
RINGED PINS
PENNING
BOW BROOCHES
LAVA QUERNS
POTTERY
JEWELLERY
DIRHAM
SILKS
COWRIE SHELL

ABOVE
101 The geographical range of York's Viking Age contacts, as shown by the foreign objects found at Coppergate.

BELOW
102 Cooking pot of Torksey-type ware, tenth century, showing exterior (*right*) and interior (*left*). Height 12.2cm.

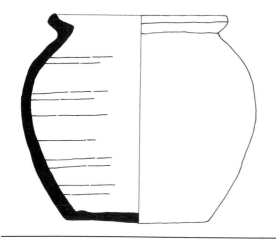

protein in the diet. Oysters were eaten in substantial quantities, as they had been in the Roman period and were to be up to the nineteenth century. Other shellfish, including cockles, mussels and winkles, were also gathered, but in smaller numbers. A wide range of fish species has been identified, thanks to an extensive programme of sieving the excavated soil, during which twelve and a half tons of earth was sieved down to a fineness of one millimetre. In addition to the big fish such as cod, whose vertebrae are so large that they can be spotted during the normal recovery of finds by hand, many thousands of tiny bones were found in this way. Freshwater species included pike, roach, rudd, bream and perch, and sea-fishing brought in herring, haddock, flat-fish, ling, horse mackerel and cod. Smelt, eels and salmon were also represented—they may have been caught at sea, in estuarine waters or in the rivers. Iron fish hooks discovered at Coppergate suggest the occupants caught some of the marine fish themselves on long lines (104 *a* and *b*) and as well as harbouring cargo vessels from Scandinavia

103 A tenth-century storage vessel of Torksey-type ware. Height 44cm.

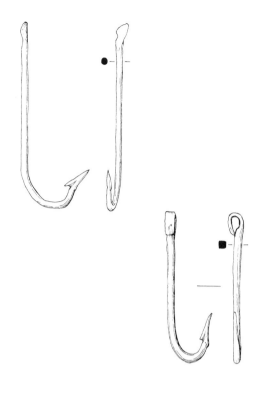

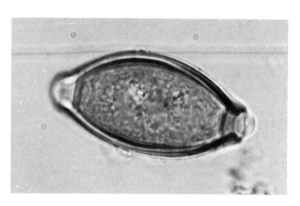

TOP
104 Iron fish-hooks from Viking Age levels. Lengths
(*a*) 5cm (*b*) 4cm.

ABOVE
105 Egg of the human intestinal parasite the
whip-worm, from a Viking Age cess pit. Length 55μ
(0.055mm).

and the Continent, York was probably also a fishing port. Other fishing was probably done with traps or nets, but remains of these were not found.

Other marine delicacies may have appeared occasionally on the dining tables of Jorvik— remains of guillemots were among the bird bones recovered, and it is quite possible that they are food remains. The most common bird bones were those of chickens, which provided both meat and eggs; wild geese and duck were also common together with a few examples of the common crane (now a rare vagrant), and wildfowling must have been a regular activity. Several hawks, falcons and other birds of prey were represented among the bird bones, but not goshawk or peregrine falcon, two of the classic hawking birds trained for the hunt, and it seems that the kestrel, red kite, buzzard and sea eagle (unusual so far from the coast), together with other birds, particularly the raven, were probably just scavengers, picking up scraps of carrion from among the domestic rubbish lying rotting in the backyards. Although several of these species are today quite rare in Britain, and are found only in remote areas, to the citizens of Viking Age York they were commonplace. Other birds included moorland species such as golden plover, grey plover, and black grouse, and these too were eaten along with wood pigeons and lapwing.

Fruit stones, nuts, pips and seeds give insights into other sectors of the diet. Apples, sloes, various kinds of small plums, bilberries, blackberries and raspberries made up the bulk of the fruit intake, and both hazel-nuts and walnuts were available. Vegetables included carrots, parsnips, celery and possibly brassicas, and among herbs and spices in use were dill and coriander. Other plant remains which may have had a culinary use include linseed and hempseed, both of which produce an edible oil in small quantities. Particularly from cess pits there came microscopic remains of grain and bran concretions, and the cereals represented included wheat, rye, barley and oats. The bran concretions contained significant amounts of the poisonous weed corncockle, enough to have given consumers a stomach-ache.

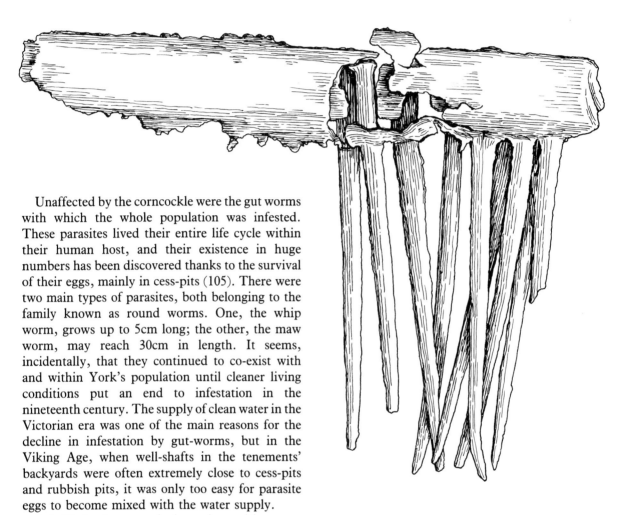

Unaffected by the corncockle were the gut worms with which the whole population was infested. These parasites lived their entire life cycle within their human host, and their existence in huge numbers has been discovered thanks to the survival of their eggs, mainly in cess-pits (105). There were two main types of parasites, both belonging to the family known as round worms. One, the whip worm, grows up to 5cm long; the other, the maw worm, may reach 30cm in length. It seems, incidentally, that they continued to co-exist with and within York's population until cleaner living conditions put an end to infestation in the nineteenth century. The supply of clean water in the Victorian era was one of the main reasons for the decline in infestation by gut-worms, but in the Viking Age, when well-shafts in the tenements' backyards were often extremely close to cess-pits and rubbish pits, it was only too easy for parasite eggs to become mixed with the water supply.

It is likely that a weak, home-brewed beer was commonly drunk; although no hops have yet been recognised in the Coppergate samples, they have been found on other Viking Age sites. Imported Rhine wine appeared at least occasionally at meal-times, if the evidence of German pottery wine vessels is taken at face value (**92**, p. 81), and there was probably also mead, a stronger, honey-based drink—a swarm of bees found amid the remains of a portable hive or skep may have supplied the basic ingredients for this. Honey was also important as the only sweetener available.

107 Fragmentary iron wool-comb. Tenth century. Length 15cm.

As well as preparing the family's meals, the women of the house were also responsible for making many of their clothes. It is likely that, apart from their leather shoes, people's wardrobes included garments made of skins and furs, such as cloaks, gloves and hats, although none have been found. Linen garments were also probably common, but linen is not normally preserved in York's soils. Both flax seeds and hemp fruits have been preserved, however, indicating that linen and hempen cloth may have been produced. Imported silks were also occasionally used for clothing, as a silk cap vividly demonstrates (**106**, p. 112): it shows signs of repair where draw-strings were originally attached, and was obviously a treasured possession or even, perhaps, a status symbol.

The most common items of clothing to survive are woollens, and there is evidence that many of these were homespun; the archaeological finds illustrate many stages in their production. A comb with iron teeth was first used to comb impurities from the wool and to prepare it for spinning (107). Spindle-whorls, the perforated weights made of animal bone, pottery sherds, stone or occasionally lead, which weighted the hand-held spindles on which the woollen thread was spun out, are among the commonest objects found in the excavation and suggest that spinning was a daily occupation (108).

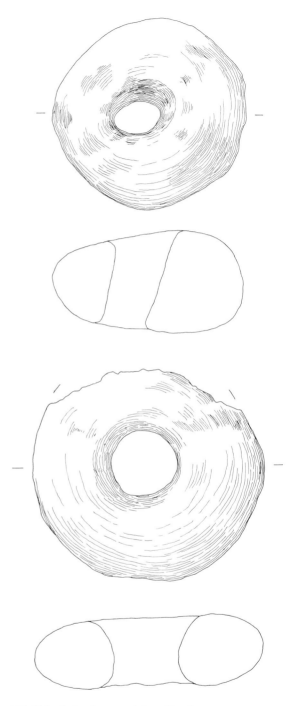

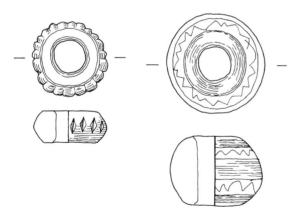

108 Viking Age stone spindle-whorls. Diameter (*a*) 2.2cm (*b*) 2.9cm.

109 Baked clay loom weights. Tenth century. Diameter (*a*) 9.5cm (*b*) 11.5cm.

|1cm|

110 Tenth-century woollen sock.

After the woollen thread had been spun, it could be woven into lengths of cloth using a hand-loom, which was made largely of wood. No pieces from one have yet been identified for certain among the surviving wood, but the woollen threads suspended from the top of the loom were held in position by fired-clay loom-weights which look like ring-doughnuts, and several of these have been found (109).

The Coppergate site is not remarkable for its spindle-whorls or loom-weights, but it has yielded the greatest selection of textile remains ever recovered from a Viking Age site in England. There is only one complete garment, a woollen sock, patched in antiquity, made in a technique called single-needle knitting which in appearance looks like close-textured crochet work (110). This is a technique still well known in Scandinavia—a visitor to an exhibition of Coppergate finds stopped in front of a display case containing bone needles, and remarked that she had seen identical needles being used for single-needle knitting far up in the Swedish dales, where it is called *nålbindning*. Indeed, it seems quite

likely that this form of textile was brought to York by the Scandinavians.

All the other pieces of textile are fragments of garments, mostly plain pieces without any clue to what they formed a part of. Together they show the wide range of weaving techniques which were used to create a variety of patterned effects in the cloth, which itself varied considerably in its appearance, from the quite coarse to the very fine (111). The cloth fragments all appear a dull brown colour when excavated and cleaned; laboratory analysis is required to prove that they were originally a blaze of colour. Reds, greens, blues, yellows, blacks and all shades in between could be produced using a range of natural dye substances such as the plants madder (red), woad (blue) and weld (yellow), either singly or in combination. All these plants have been identified among the botanical remains from the site, and it seems that as well as producing their own textiles the Coppergate residents also dyed them. Dye-stuffs

99

1cm

111 A variety of Viking Age woollen textiles.

had been largely unrecognised before the programme of analysis on the Coppergate textiles, which has considerably added to our picture of what the people of York actually looked like as they went about their business.

There are perhaps two clues to how garments were decorated. A small, square plate of antler with a hole at each corner is a type of object used in tablet weaving (112). This is a method of forming a complex coloured braid or decorated edgestrip, in which threads of different colours are attached to each corner and the pattern created by revolving the tablet and threads through ninety, one hundred and eighty, two hundred and seventy or three hundred and sixty degrees as another thread is woven through them (113). These tablet-woven braids could be very elaborate and opulent; they sometimes included gold thread, and one short fragment of such a thread, which may have embellished an item of clothing, was found in the excavation.

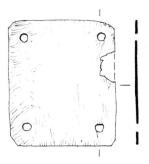

ABOVE
112 Perforated antler plate, used in tablet weaving. Height 2.7cm.

BELOW
113 Explanatory diagram of how tablet weaving is done.

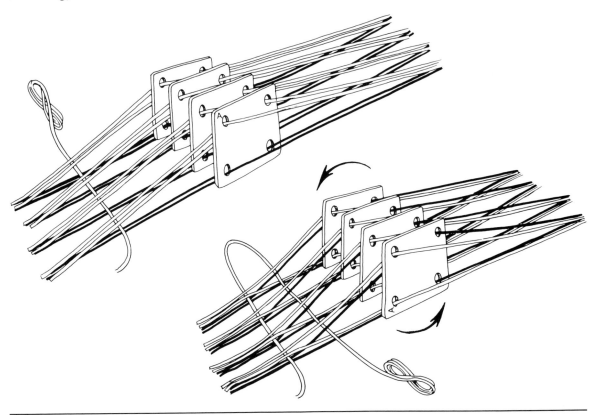

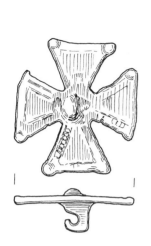

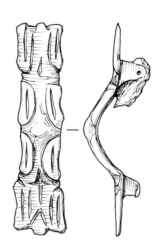

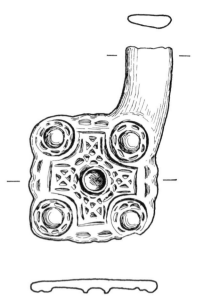

TOP LEFT
114 Bronze cross-brooch from Germany, found in tenth-century deposits. Height 3.4cm.

TOP CENTRE
115 Copper alloy bow or caterpillar brooch, probably made in the Low Countries, and found in tenth-century levels. Length 5.4cm.

TOP RIGHT
116a Terminal plate from a Pictish penannular brooch of copper alloy, made in Scotland, and found in tenth-century levels. Length 5cm.

ABOVE
116b How a penannular brooch was worn.

In addition to providing a rare chance to look at Viking Age costume, Coppergate was also rich in jewellery, although most of it was of the mass-produced rather than the up-market variety. Indeed, many of the pieces were probably made in the metalsmiths' workshops, and this seems particularly true of the disc brooches which, with strap-ends, are the commonest type of jewellery found. These disc brooches vary in size, the smallest being about 2.5cm in diameter, and the largest 7cm. Most are made of lead alloy, one group with near identical decoration are made in copper alloy, and there is a single example in silver. Their decoration covers the range or ornamentation popular in Anglo-Scandinavian England: intricately knotted, unnaturally drawn animals (61), simple geometric shapes, cross motifs or stylised plant motifs (60) make up the craftsmen's basic repertoire. All these brooches had a pin and catch plate on their back, and could have been worn either purely for their decorative effect or to pin together two garments or pieces of garment. They were probably worn by both men and women. They were not the only type of brooch in use, however, for several foreign brooches were also found, including a copper-alloy cross-brooch from Germany (114) and a so-called 'caterpillar' brooch from the Low Countries (115). There was also part of a penannular brooch from Scotland (116a), which works on a different

principle from the others, but which could also hold together a cloak, in the way shown in (116b).

The other most common class of jewellery discovered was a series of strap-ends, usually made of metal (copper alloy, iron or, in one most unusual example, lead) but occasionally of bone/antler. These objects were attached to the ends of the straps and belts which held various garments in place in order to stop them from fraying. The metal ones were usually split at their upper ends, and when the strap was inserted it was clasped with tiny rivets as the split ends were pressed together (117). Some of the bone ones worked in the same way, while others had a hole cut out at their upper end through which the strap could be threaded (85). As with the disc brooches, their decoration includes animal ornament, in the form of stylised animal heads at the ends of some (118), and geometric and interlace designs (119).

BELOW LEFT
117 Tenth-century openwork strap-end of copper alloy. Length 5.8cm.

BELOW CENTRE
118 Lead-alloy strap-end, tenth century, with stylised animal head terminal. Length 4.9cm.

BELOW RIGHT
119 Copper-alloy strap-end, tenth century, with knot and animal head decoration. Length 4.8cm.

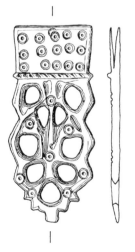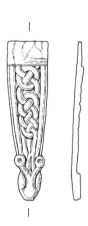

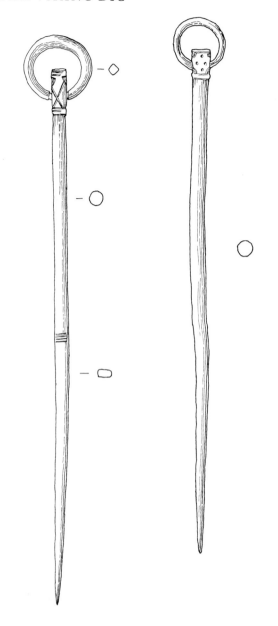

Other items of jewellery found in smaller numbers include dress or cloak pins of Irish origin, called 'ringed pins' for obvious reasons, which were simply stuck through the garment to fasten it together (120 *a* and *b*), and the more puzzling items called 'garter hooks' (121 *a* and *b*) which may have held up socks or 'stockings', or may have had some other function. Finger rings were relatively common, and include several of very plain form and others made of plaited wires (122 *a–d*). These are all of base metals—lead, bronze and even iron—but there was also one silver ring with a bezel decorated with an animal design (123). There were also rings of amber and jet, and these two substances were also made into pendants and beads, all of this activity taking place on the site (**81**, p. 87). Glass beads were also commonly worn, ranging from large multi-coloured examples down to minute ones which were probably sewn on to the clothing rather than being part of a string (**124**, p. 112).

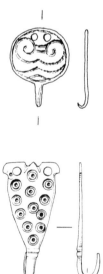

ABOVE LEFT
120 *a* and *b* Tenth-century copper alloy ringed pins. from Ireland. Length (*a*) 14.1cm (*b*) 13.3cm.

ABOVE
121 *a* and *b* Copper alloy garter hooks, tenth century. Length (*a*) 2.1cm (*b*) 3.1cm.

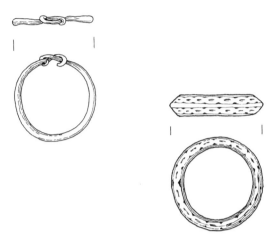

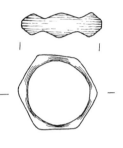

122 *a–d* Copper alloy (*a–c*) and lead alloy (*d*) Viking Age finger rings. Internal diameters (*a*) 1.8cm (*b*) 1.8cm (*c*) 1.7cm (*d*) 1.6cm.

123 Late ninth/tenth-century silver ring, its bezel decorated with animal interlace. Diameter of bezel 8 mm.

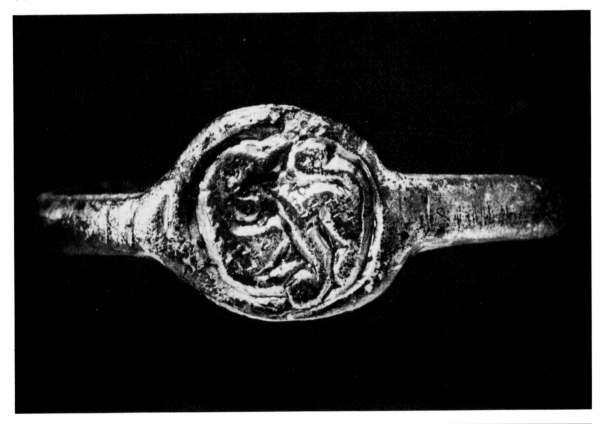

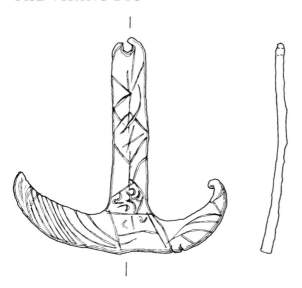

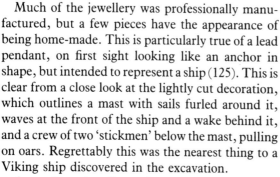

Much of the jewellery was professionally manufactured, but a few pieces have the appearance of being home-made. This is particularly true of a lead pendant, on first sight looking like an anchor in shape, but intended to represent a ship (125). This is clear from a close look at the lightly cut decoration, which outlines a mast with sails furled around it, waves at the front of the ship and a wake behind it, and a crew of two 'stickmen' below the mast, pulling on oars. Regrettably this was the nearest thing to a Viking ship discovered in the excavation.

Apart from jewellery, there were several other items commonly worn or carried about. Combs, made from antler or, occasionally, bone, were found in considerable numbers, and were clearly much in use—perhaps not surprising when lice and nits were probably common problems (126). The combs could be carried in carefully fitting bone combcases, some of which had a small hole drilled through them at one end so that they could be

TOP
125 Lead-alloy ship pendant. Tenth century. Height 5.7cm.

OPPOSITE
126 Tenth-century antler and bone products—combs and a comb-case. Scale measures 5cm.

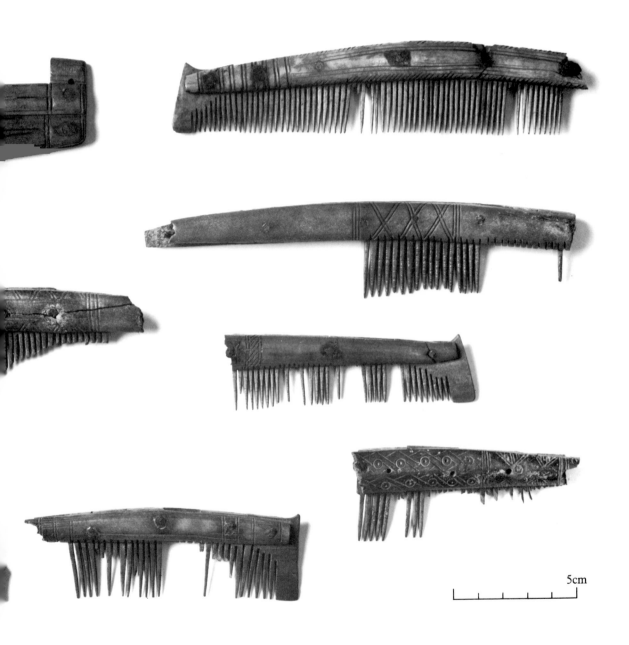

5cm

attached to a belt or strap by a thong. Most people probably carried a small pocket knife, averaging about 12cm long, with a wooden or bone handle fixed around an iron tang which ran directly into the blade. Surprisingly in these moist conditions the handles survive only occasionally, but the knives themselves are among the commonest objects recovered (127). Knives were useful in many ways on the domestic front from cutting up food to severing knotted strappings, but some more un-usual types probably had very specialised functions in craft industry. Another item frequently carried, at least by merchants and traders, was a set of folding scales, used to weigh out silver when the clipped fragments of coins or fractions of ingots changed hands as payment for goods. When

assembled, a bronze pan hung on three chains from each arm of the scales, but the arms could be folded up for easy carriage (128). A small selection of lead weights would also have been carried, and several examples of these were also found.

Keys were likewise fairly common, and were probably carried about for safe-keeping. Some are variations on the twist-key form standard today but many others are for the now superseded barrel padlock (129). This took the form of a cylinder within which splayed metal prongs held the lock shut (130). To open it the prongs had to be pushed together at the centre and this was achieved by inserting a special key with a foot-plate at an angle to the stem (131). In the foot-plate was a hole of a shape suitable to fit around all the prongs when they were extended and which would then force them together as the key was pushed further in. The keys were probably not for the doors of the buildings although these might sometimes have been locked; an appropriate lock case has been found in Viking Age layers just seventy metres away below Lloyds Bank in Pavement. It seems more probable that they were used to secure chests and boxes in which household, personal and commercial valuables could be stored. No chests remained to be discovered, but a number of iron hinges, hasps and bindings may have originally belonged to them.

One side of Viking Age life which was *not* well represented among the finds was warfare. The citizens of Viking Age York were accustomed to a world of much personal and political violence, and they would have had weapons at home as a matter of course, but because weapons were valuable, they passed from father to son or from vanquished to victor, and were not normally thrown away or easily lost. Even if broken, the value of their metal content ensured that they were bartered back to the weapon-smith in part-exchange as scrap metal. The archaeological evidence for weaponry is slight, but includes a leather sword-scabbard, and parts of sword handles. Among these is a remarkable example made from whalebone (132). Although found in a layer dated to the Norman period, its shape suggests that it might have been made in the

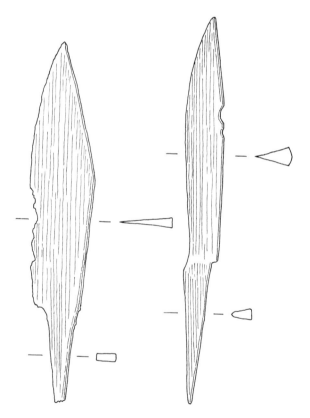

127 Viking Age iron knives. Length (*a*) 11.3cm (*b*) 10.5cm.

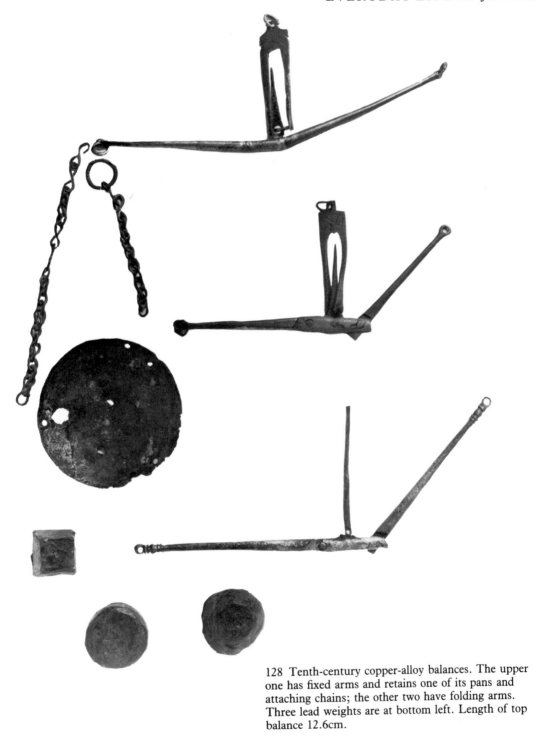

128 Tenth-century copper-alloy balances. The upper
one has fixed arms and retains one of its pans and
attaching chains; the other two have folding arms.
Three lead weights are at bottom left. Length of top
balance 12.6cm.

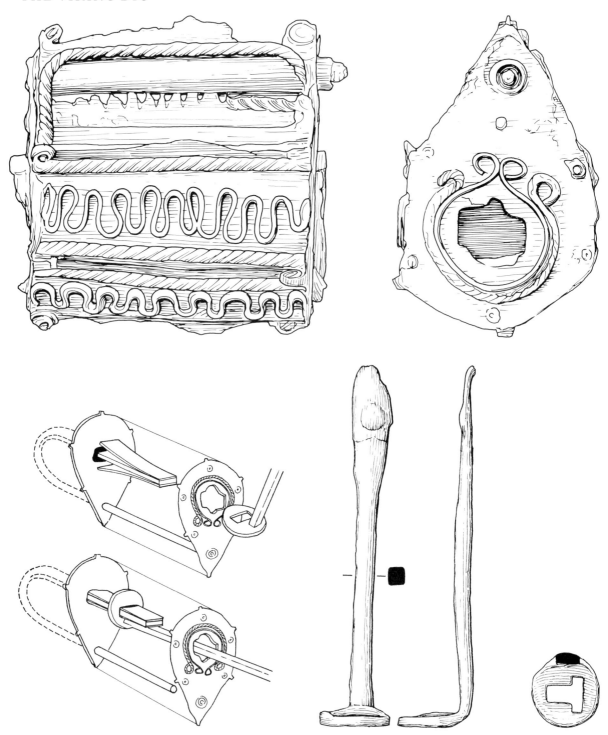

Viking Age. Other more ambiguous finds include several knives which are perhaps for defence rather than domestic use, and a number of arrow heads which may have been intended for hunting rather than fighting (133). Spurs, which are a relatively rare find in Viking Age England, could have had a military use, but are better thought of as the personal equipment of someone wealthy enough to own a horse (134). Other evidence for transport is lacking, although carts, wagons and, in winter, sledges were all probably used.

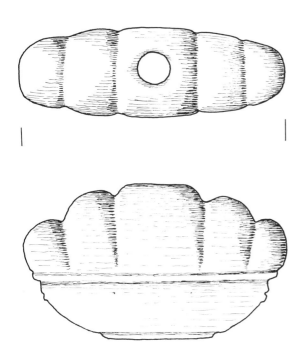

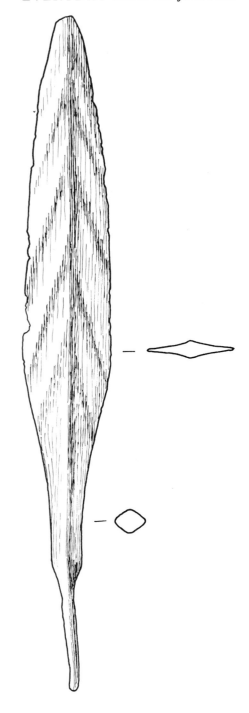

OPPOSITE TOP
129 Iron barrel padlock, tenth century. Length 8.6cm.

OPPOSITE LEFT
130 The mechanism of a barrel padlock.

OPPOSITE RIGHT
131 Iron key for a barrel padlock. Length 9.3cm.

ABOVE
132 Whalebone sword pommel, probably of Viking Age date. Length 7.2cm.

133 Iron arrow head, tenth century. Length 15.4cm.

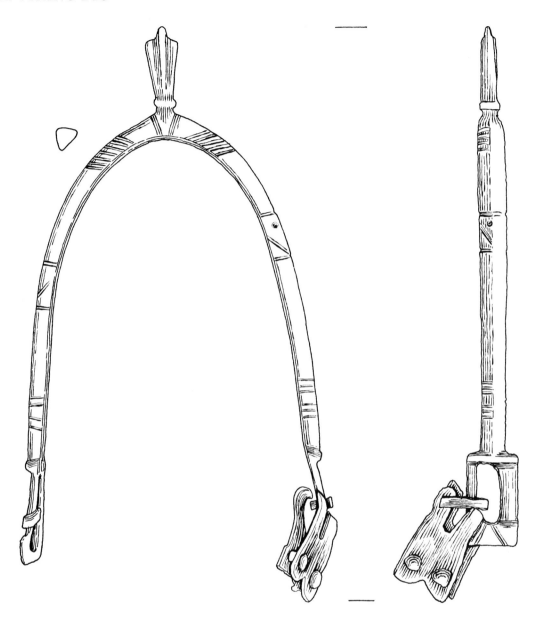

ABOVE
134 Iron spur, tenth century. Length 14.5cm.

OPPOSITE
106 Tenth-century silk cap from 5–7 Coppergate
(p. 88).

124 Viking Age glass beads (p. 104).

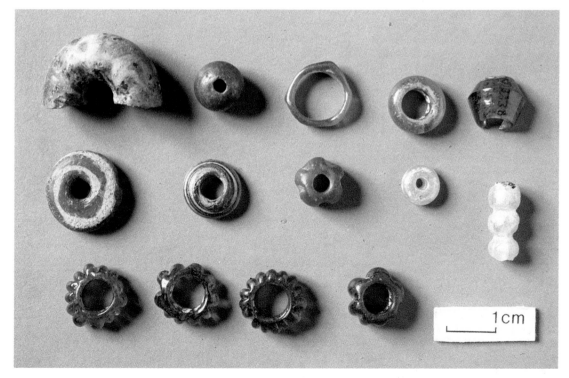

The final area of Anglo-Scandinavian life which the Coppergate finds illuminate is the leisure activities of York's citizens. One seasonal pursuit was ice-skating, as several dozen ice-skates testify (135). They were made from the foot bones of horses and cattle, which were shaped to a point at what was to be the front end and flattened on the underside. It was mainly the weight of the wearer which kept the skates in place, and the feet were never removed from the surface of the ice, but some skates had a hole in their rear end where a peg with ties attached to the skater's boot could be lodged, and there might be another hole at the front where a fastening could be made. Propulsion was gained by a single pole, like a ski-stick. Similar skates were in use in Norway until the nineteenth century, and they were obviously very effective. In the twelfth century a Norman writer, William fitz Stephen, described how the younger elements enjoyed themselves at the frozen Moorfields, outside London.

OPPOSITE
136 Playing pieces of chalk and antler displayed on a modern *hnefatafl* board.

156 Glazed relief tiles, probably of eleventh/twelfth-century date (p. 126).

ABOVE
135 Tenth-century ice skates made from animal bones: the polished surface of each is the underside.

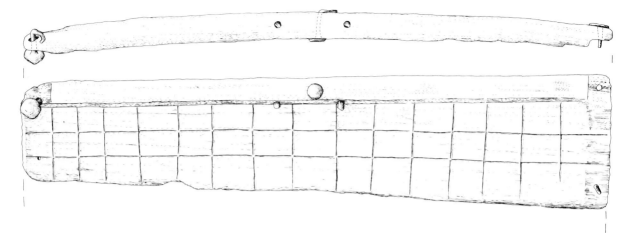

'. . . Others, more skilled at winter sports, put on their feet the shin-bones of animals, binding them firmly round their ankles, and, holding poles shod with iron in their hands, which they strike from time to time against the ice, they are propelled swift as a bird in flight or a bolt shot from an engine of war. Sometimes, by mutual consent, two of them run against each other in this way from a great distance, and, lifting their poles, each tilts against the other. Either one or both fall, not without some bodily injury, for, as they fall, they are carried along a great way beyond each other by the impetus of their run, and whenever the ice comes in contact with their heads, it scrapes off the skin utterly. Often a leg or an arm is broken, if the victim falls with it underneath him; but theirs is an age greedy for glory, youth yearns for victory, and exercises itself in mock combats in order to carry itself more bravely in real battles.'

When the rivers and the adjacent marshland (the 'ings') of York became ice-bound, similar horseplay probably occurred, but skating may also have been a quick and practical way of getting around town. The frequency of these skates in the Anglo-Scandinavian and Norman levels is one of the principal indicators that the climate then was slightly different from today, when it takes an exceptionally cold winter to create extensive tracts of ice in and around the city.

ABOVE
137 Fragmentary wooden gaming board, tenth century. Length 52.5cm.

BELOW
138 Bone and jet dice. Length (a) 8mm (b) 1.1cm.

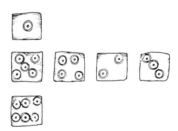

Admittedly it was easier for the rivers to freeze solid when they were wider and shallower, as they were then, before their channels were narrowed by building out into the rivers and reclaiming their edges as happened increasingly from the twelfth/ thirteenth century onwards. Nonetheless, the skates suggest the winters may on average have been a few degrees colder than they are at present, and perhaps York enjoyed a more continental climate than it does today, with colder winters and hotter summers.

There are also finds which give us a rare and precious insight into the pastimes and entertainments of the people of Anglo-Scandinavian York. The largest single group is playing pieces, used in a variety of games to mark the players' position or score. Some are simply pieces of pottery, crudely shaped as required, others are more carefully manufactured from antler or stone (**136**). One group of chalk pieces, found close together, seemed to

make up parts of two sets, one distinguished by a coating of red pigment. Sets like this were used in board games, and part of a wooden playing board, a most unusual discovery, was also found at Copper-gate (**137**). Made of oak, with a raised strip nailed along the edges to prevent pieces falling off, the squares were marked out crudely with roughly incised lines. The board, presumably originally square, was fifteen squares wide, but only three ranks were preserved. What game was played on it can only be guessed at; contrary to popular opinion, chess was probably *not* played in England in the tenth century, and a Scandinavian game such as *hnefatafl* is perhaps more likely. *Hnefatafl*, like draughts or chess, was a game of skill for two people, and needed no props apart from the board and two sets of playing pieces, but dice were also quite common finds, and show that games of chance were also popular (**138**).

An unexpected bonus was the discovery of several

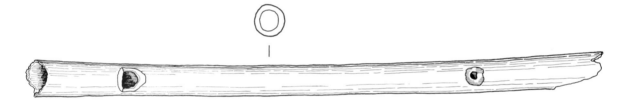

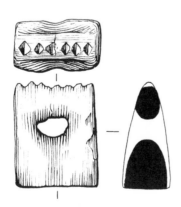

ABOVE
139 Viking Age bone whistle. Length 18.1cm.

LEFT
140 Wooden lyre bridge, tenth century. Height 2.7cm.

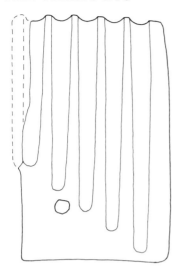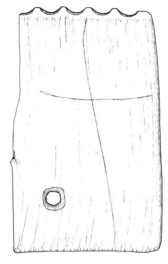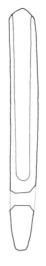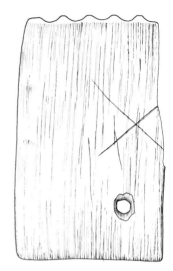

musical instruments. Whistles made from the leg bones of birds are a well-known type and did not cause much surprise (139), but the wooden bridge for a six-stringed lyre is very much rarer (140). An even rarer musical instrument, indeed a unique discovery, is a set of panpipes made from a small slab of boxwood (141). Holes were bored to different depths into the slab, and then the top of each hole was bevelled slightly to allow the player to sound the individual notes more easily and comfortably (142). (Another hole bored through the instrument near one corner has nothing to do with music making, but is there to take a thong by which the pipes could be hung up.) Remarkably, after a careful removal of the soil which had become lodged in the surviving five holes, a five-note scale running from top A to top E could still be sounded, and simple tunes played on the pipes. With the exception of the simple whistles they are probably the only Viking Age musical instrument still in working order, and their unique preservation shows perhaps more than any other object the sort of detailed knowledge of everyday life which the Coppergate excavation has provided.

ABOVE
141 Fragmentary wooden panpipes, tenth century. Height 9.5cm.

RIGHT
142 Playing the tenth-century panpipes.

8
Medieval Developments and the Viking Revival

William the Conqueror and his invading Norman army did not reach York until 1068. William must have been wary of the city's tradition of independence and its close Scandinavian links, but after building an earth and timber castle there he moved southwards again. The castle did not overawe the people of York; its garrison was attacked early in 1069, and William returned to the city, put down the insurgents, and built a second castle.

A renewed anti-Norman Northumbrian uprising in the summer of 1069 was fuelled by the arrival in the Humber estuary of a Danish fleet commanded by the Danish king's sons. The English heir to the throne, Edgar, joined the rebels, as did Gospatric the earl of Northumbria and Waltheof, son of a former earl. The Norman garrison of York was defeated, the city was seized, and the north of England seemed set to slip from William's grasp. William's response was a swift and decisive march north again, and on his approach the Danes evacuated York, leaving William to celebrate Christmas 1069 in the city. Although the Danish king and his fleet were to plunder York in 1075, the threat of 1069 was never repeated, and York's political links with Scandinavia were gradually severed.

On the Coppergate site the destruction of archaeological remains caused by modern foundations obviously had its worst impact on the uppermost layers, and the picture of the site's development after about A D 1000 becomes gradually less complete as modern disturbance takes an increasing toll. Nevertheless, the Coppergate excavation still provides the most comprehensive picture available of everyday life in medieval York.

At the street frontage the sunken buildings erected at the end of the tenth century or in the early years of the eleventh were the latest to survive on all except one of the tenements where the rear wall of one building and the front of another behind it were preserved (143 **A** and **B**). These walls were represented only by foundation beams, in one case (**A**) underpinned by other shorter beams at right angles (144), in the other with remnants of what look like a plank floor beside them. In the absence of a dendrochronological date for the felling of these timbers, dating the fragmentary buildings precisely is difficult. The underlying sunken buildings seem to have gone out of use in the first half of the eleventh century, and on an important frontage site they would normally have been replaced immediately. On the other hand, the few broadly datable objects found in the same layers as the upper buildings might equally well suggest that they may belong to the early Norman period, in the late eleventh century. Whichever side of the Norman Conquest these structures were built, the backyards behind them remained open areas in the way they had done before.

Although it is recorded that the Norman Con-

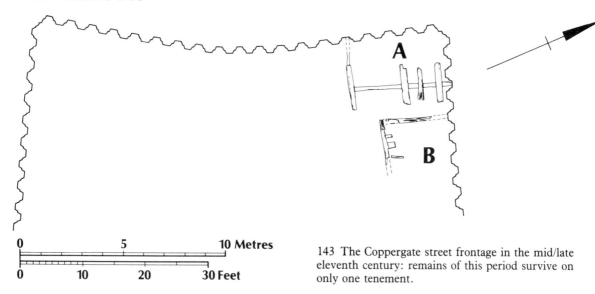

143 The Coppergate street frontage in the mid/late eleventh century: remains of this period survive on only one tenement.

144 Eleventh-century building (**A** on 143) with cross-braced foundation beams. Scale measures 50cm.

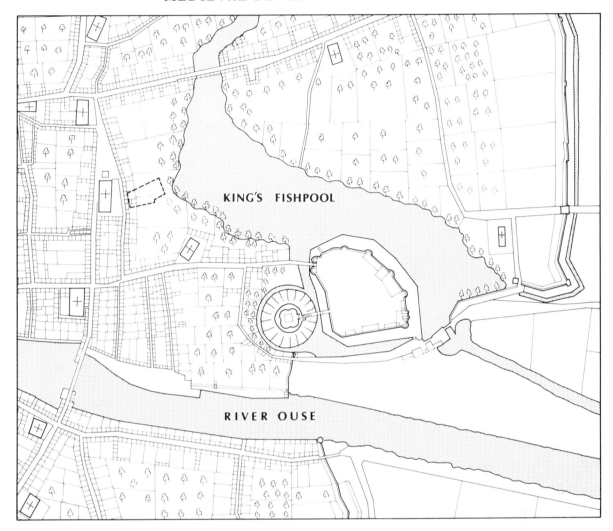

KING'S FISHPOOL

RIVER OUSE

quest of York led to widespread devastation, with a great fire in 1069 consuming the area around the castle including, presumably, Coppergate which is less than two hundred metres from it, no clear signs of this disaster were found in the excavation. But there was one substantial feature which most probably owed its origin to the Normans, and to the precautions they took in attempts to make their castle impregnable. Their defensive measures included digging ditches around the castle, and then damming the River Foss and diverting its flow into the newly created moat. This damming of the river

145 A detail from James Archer's plan of York, c.1682, showing the Coppergate site, its surrounds and the King's Fishpool.

also resulted in the formation of a large lake, known in the Middle Ages as the King's Fishpool, which built up behind the dam (145). The encroaching waters threatened to overwhelm the lower-lying parts of the tenements at Coppergate, and it was probably to counter the likelihood of flood that a dump of soil up to two metres in thickness was laid down there. This brought the backyards up above

the new water-level, lessened the angle at which they sloped, and also had beneficial effects on the archaeology of the site, for it neatly separated the medieval levels from those of Viking Age date, and prevented the earlier ones from being badly cut about by medieval pits.

If it is correct to suggest that this dump was put down in the years immediately after the Norman Conquest, then it becomes possible that a human skeleton lying in a shallow grave immediately below it was a victim of the unsettled times which followed the conquest (146). The skeleton was that of a woman aged over forty-five, who had suffered badly with hip trouble. Why she should have been buried here is a mystery since at this date churchyard burial was usual for all except excommunicants and felons, and even they are unlikely to have been buried in the backyard. Perhaps she was a victim of foul play whose body was disposed of secretly.

As well as large amounts of animal bone and pottery, the dump of soil contained a wide cross-section of objects, including horseshoes, quern-stones, spindle whorls, dice, pins, needles, combs, whetstones, keys, knives, and other domestic paraphernalia. This suggests that the dump consisted of soil collected from an area in the heart of the city, but its exact source is not known. Several iron arrow heads were found lying on the surface directly above the dump, suggesting that the area was used by archers for target practice in the twelfth century (147 *a* and *b*).

In about AD 1180 a building with walls at least partly constructed of stone was erected near the front of the north tenement (148 **C**, 149). Up to three courses of limestone rubble blocks survived, forming the lowest courses of the rear wall; when completely exposed they were seen to rest upon a wider raft of cobbles (150). When these were eventually removed in their turn it was found that they were not the only foundation for the wall, for underneath, in a trench, lay a raft of massive oak boughs (151). They were there because the builders had recognised what was to be the major problem confronting every builder on the site from that time up to the present day—the problem of ensuring secure foundations for a heavy structure in wet soils which were likely to move under pressure, resulting in the collapse of walls resting upon them. The answer adopted here was extravagant in its use of timber, and many of the later medieval structures rested on clusters or rows of piles, a more economical way of building. Each of these methods is of great value to the archaeologist, for so long as the timber used is oak, these timbers are normally sufficiently large to allow tree-ring dating which, as in this instance, may give precise information about when the structure was put up. With all archaeological deposits above it destroyed by modern cellars, it is impossible to say how long the building stood or what purpose it served. The likelihood, however, is that it was a house, and that it stood for some time, perhaps a century or more.

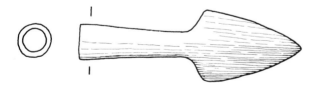

OPPOSITE
146 The skeleton of a middle-aged woman found below the Norman flood defences.

ABOVE
147 Iron arrow heads, twelfth century. Length (*a*) 6cm (*b*) 5.8cm.

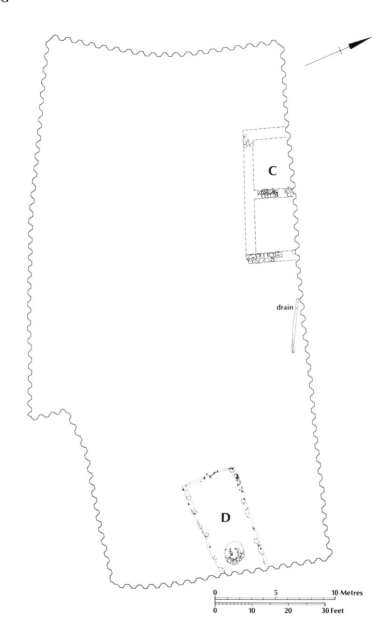

148 The Coppergate site—features surviving from the
twelfth century.

149 Late twelfth-century building (**C** on 148). Scale measures 2m.

When the only remaining parts of a medieval building are its foundations or a few courses of stonework, it is still often possible to gain some idea of its original appearance by taking into account the medieval buildings which stand to this day. These show that although it may be a few courses of stone which survive, it is more than likely that most buildings were constructed in what is known as timber-framed or half-timber tradition, in which substantial timber uprights, horizontals and angled bracing beams make up the principal structural elements. The spaces between these timbers were in-filled with panels of lighter material such as wattle daubed with clay or plaster. Stone walls, when they occurred, were often only dwarf walls, a few courses

high, providing a stable and dry foundation for the timberwork above, and that seems the most likely reconstruction for this late Norman building.

Immediately behind the building was a barrel-lined pit, perhaps a well, and there were several other unusual features in the sloping back yard. A squared and hollowed beam of wood with a plank cover served as a drain, channelling water down the slope, although for what reason is not known, as it both started and finished abruptly (148). Near it at

150 Wall of late twelfth-century building (**C** on 148),
resting on a raft of cobbles, with a barrel well beyond.
Scale measures 1m.

151 Horizontal tree-trunks supporting the cobble raft foundation for the late twelfth-century building (**C** on 148). Scale measures 1m.

one point was a pit in whose upper surface lay a complete wattlework hurdle (152). The pointed ends of the more substantial members showed that originally it had stood upright, forming a screen, and perhaps it is not too fanciful to interpret it as giving a degree of privacy to a cess pit. Other pits at this level certainly were cess pits, as toilet seats made from a single plank with a hole of appropriate diameter at the centre were found abandoned in them (153).

The only building at the rear of these tenements in the twelfth century was built in the wattlework style which had been popular over two centuries earlier (148 **D**, 154). Rebuilt at least once, after a fire, it

152 Wattlework hurdle lying collapsed over a twelfth-century pit. Scale measures 50cm.

seems to have been a bakery, for inside it were several circular ovens (155), as well as many fragments of lava quern-stones which were used for grinding grain.

Although few traces of Norman period buildings survive, one group of finds from the associated layers may provide a clue to their internal decoration. The objects are square ceramic tiles fired a reddish colour but covered with a greenish glaze, with a variety of geometric patterns raised in relief on their front face (**156**, p. 113). The patterns include diamond shapes, circles and chevrons. On their plain rear faces are indentations made to help them bed firmly into a mortar base. Tiles of this type are unusual, although they have been found on a few sites widely spread throughout England. Often they are found in churches and indeed the only similar tiles in York were discovered in All Saints' Church, Pavement, immediately opposite the excavation, in 1953. It is possible that the tiles found in the excavation originally decorated the church, and somehow eventually got discarded on to the tene-ments opposite; or it may be that the occupants of Coppergate admired the church's decoration and beautified their own homes with similar tiles. In either case, they are a useful addition to the small quantity of such tiles known from England, and are among the earliest medieval tiles known in the country.

153 Twelfth-century toilet seat fallen into a cess pit. Scale measures 20cm.

ABOVE
154 Twelfth-century wattle-walled 'bakery' at the rear of the site, (**D** on 148), with the circular impression of an already excavated oven at bottom left. Scale measures 2m.

OPPOSITE
163 Medieval gold finger ring with a pearl and amethyst setting (p. 136).

173 Tile-lined channel beside medieval building (**J** on 157, p. 145). Scale measures 10cm.

OPPOSITE
179 Jorvik Viking Centre—the reconstructed waterfront.

ABOVE
155 Oven in the twelfth-century 'bakery' (**D** on 148) with rubble base and dome of wattle and daub. Scale measures 20cm.

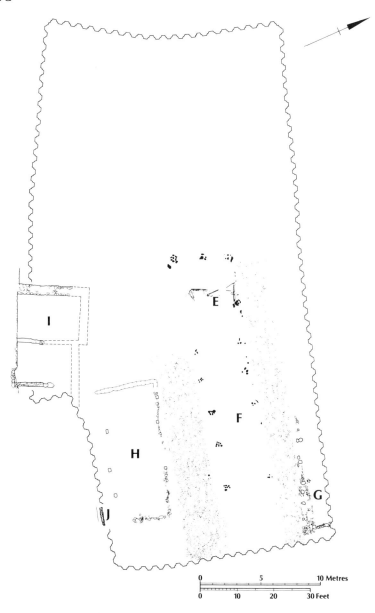

157 The Coppergate site—features surviving from the
thirteenth/fourteenth centuries, excavated before the
insertion of the perimeter shoring. Nothing from this
period remained in the western half of the site.

From the thirteenth century onwards there was an expansion in the built-up area within the four excavated tenements, with structures now being erected further down the slope towards the River Foss. This expansion did not follow a fairly uniform layout, as the tenth-century occupation had done; instead there were variations in the sizes of the buildings, the way in which they were constructed, and where they were placed within the tenement (157).

Dating the medieval layers and structures with any sort of precision is difficult except where building foundations include timbers big enough to be suitable for tree-ring dating. Otherwise we have to rely on the changing pottery types found in and around the buildings to provide some indication of when they were put up and how long they remained in use. This is a much less precise method of dating because some pottery styles were current for long periods, and thus when pottery is the only clue to dating the dates suggested often cover a broad span

of a century or more. Likewise the small objects recovered from the medieval deposits cannot normally be used as clues to the date of the layer where they were found, except in the broadest terms. To make accurate dating even more difficult, only a small number of medieval coins was found, and because they had a much longer life in circulation than the Viking Age pennies, they are not such clear chronological indicators. One group of five late thirteenth- and early fourteenth-century silver pennies does provide a more precise indicator of date for the layer where they were found, but this is an isolated instance (158). For all these reasons, much of what follows is described in rather approximate dating terms except where there is a relevant tree-ring date.

158 Five sterlings, silver pennies from the time of Edward I (1272–1307), and Edward II (1307–27).

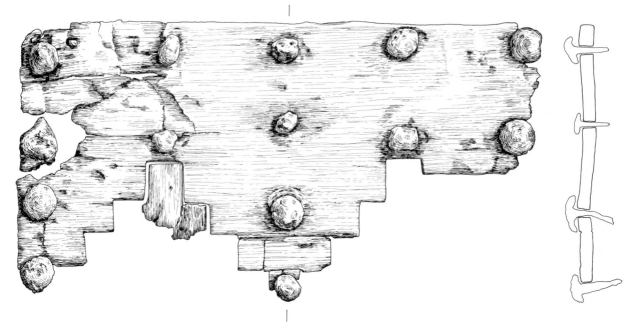

159 Early thirteenth-century building of horizontal boards supported by vertical posts (**E** on 157); the picture is complicated by many later piles supporting structures which had floors at a higher level. Scale measures 1m.

ABOVE
160 Thirteenth-century wooden casket lid with domed nails. Length 34.7cm.

One important, widespread and long-lived change in the appearance of York's buildings which took place during the thirteenth century was the re-introduction of the tiled roof. Roman buildings on the site had been roofed in standard red tiles of fired clay which provided a waterproof cover, but there was no obvious trace of roofing material during the excavation of the Viking Age and Norman period buildings, and the conclusion drawn was that they were roofed in thatch. From the thirteenth-century levels upwards, however, pieces of red, fired-clay tiles, rather thinner than the Roman ones, were found in very large numbers, occasionally with the wooden peg which held them to the roof still

preserved. The city's roofscape was probably transformed within a few decades to present the appearance still seen in parts of York today.

The earliest of the thirteenth-century buildings was found on the north-central tenement, and was dated by dendrochronology to the 1220s (157 **E**). It was a small wooden shed, with walls made of horizontal planks held in place by upright posts driven into the ground (159). There were no proper foundations. Although most of it was later destroyed by the erection of other structures, enough of the floor remained for soil samples to reveal that it had been used on at least one occasion as a grain store. From it came other tangible finds, including a wooden casket lid with a marquetry design and decoration of domed nails (160). Even more remarkable was a box lid made of rushes woven around a wooden frame, preserved in perfect condition (161).

The life-span of the shed is not known, but it must have been demolished by about 1280 when a new and larger building (157 **F**), measuring 18.4m × 3.6m, was erected over the central part of this tenement, including most of the area previously occupied by the shed. Only the foundations of this

new building survived; they consisted of clusters of oak piles driven into the ground, with rubble set in clay around their tops (162). Presumably the principal uprights along each wall rested on these pile clusters, either directly or by way of an intervening pad-stone, but no traces of either were found. Even the floor of the building had been largely cut away by later pits and wells, and the objects found within and around gave no clear indication of what the building was used for.

OPPOSITE
162 Medieval building (**F** on 157) represented by the tops of pile-cluster foundations packed with limestone rubble on the left, and pile clusters exposed in a later pit on the right. Scale measures 1m.

164 Rubble footings and post-holes of building (**G** on 157), with remnants of an alleyway beside it. Scale measures 1m.

ABOVE
161 An early thirteenth-century box lid made of plaited rushes, lying as found. Scale measures 10cm.

Unusual among these finds was a tiny gold finger ring, with a central pearl and four small amethysts forming the jewelled setting (**163**). Rings of this quality were normally carefully looked after, and are rarely found either by chance or during excavation. The style of the setting suggests a thirteenth-century date, but the sex of the wearer is in doubt—men as well as women wore such rings.

A cobbled alleyway with quite a good, even surface separated this building from the adjacent tenement to the north, where much of the central area was an open space used for pit-digging. At the river end of the excavation there was, however, a succession of buildings fronting on to the alleyway (157 **G**). These lay only partly within the excavation and their function was not obvious, but they are interesting as they show builders struggling, over a period of perhaps a century, to construct a more enduring type of building.

165 The pad-stone building (**H** on 157), with an alleyway beside it. Scales measure 2m.

166 Medieval barrel-lined well, containing an iron-bound wooden bucket. Scale measures 20cm.

In the earliest phase piled foundations were used; these were replaced by a row of rubble and tile footings, and at a later date the principal wall-posts rested in post-holes dug to receive them (164). In its final form a series of pad-stones underpinned new uprights, and at this stage the building encroached on to the alleyway. This was the latest building to occupy the site; from the time of its abandonment right through to the sixteenth century its site remained vacant.

On the other side of the pile-built structure (F) another alleyway ran down towards the River Foss. Alongside it was a large building whose main upright timbers had rested on squared pad-stones, which slowed down the onset of damp rot at their bases (157 **H**). Scanty traces of some intervening lengths of rubble foundations could also be recognised. When seen with the accompanying alley surface the wall lines were hard to distinguish in places (165), but once the alleyway had been removed, the building became quite easy to see. This building seems to belong to the thirteenth/ fourteenth century, but its function is not known.

167 Barrel staves, their hazel withy binding, and the
willow withies securing the hazel loops, in a medieval
barrel-lined well-shaft.

168 The medieval bucket after excavation, showing its iron binding, handle and link chain. Height 33cm.

Intriguingly, a small globule of mercury was recovered from its floors, suggesting that metalworkers may have operated here, although there was no trace of the furnace which they would have needed. Immediately behind the building, towards the river, there was a barrel-lined well (166). The oak staves forming the barrel were bound together with lengths of hazel withy, each of which was itself taped together with willow withy where its ends overlapped (167). When the well was excavated a particularly fine example of an iron-bound stave-built wooden bucket, complete with iron handle, swivel-ring and part of its iron link chain, was found (168).

From another pit on this tenement came a relic which shows one way in which the inhabitants spent their leisure hours. A sphere of ash wood, it is presumably a bowl used in a medieval variant of the modern game of bowls (169). Drawings of men playing with bowls exist in some thirteenth- and fourteenth-century manuscripts, although the game depicted is not similar to that played today on bowling greens throughout the country but was more like skittles, with each competitor having only one bowl. Given the marked slope of the ground at Coppergate, no game requiring a level surface could have been played here.

The southern tenement also held building remains of this period, but because of the shape of the excavated area, only the structure on the central portion of this tenement could be explored in detail by the York Excavation Group (157 **I**). This building had originally been constructed with stone walls supported by rows of densely packed wooden piles, which averaged about two metres in length (170). Later in its life additions and alterations were made to the building; new walls were inserted on less substantial foundations and cobbles were laid down as a floor or yard surface (171 **I**, 172). In this renewed condition the building probably remained in use into the fifteenth century. Behind it, and at a slight angle to it, the north wall of another building of thirteenth/fourteenth century date was recorded in the side of the excavation, before the insertion of the steel piling cut it off from view altogether (**J** on 157). This was a structure built of limestone rubble,

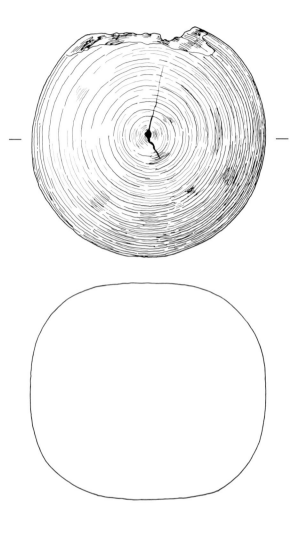

ABOVE
169 Fourteenth-century wooden bowl. Diameter 10.9cm.

OPPOSITE
170 Driven piles (the trench is the excavators', not the builders'), capped by cobble foundations, supporting a medieval stone wall (**I** on 157). Scale measures 1m.

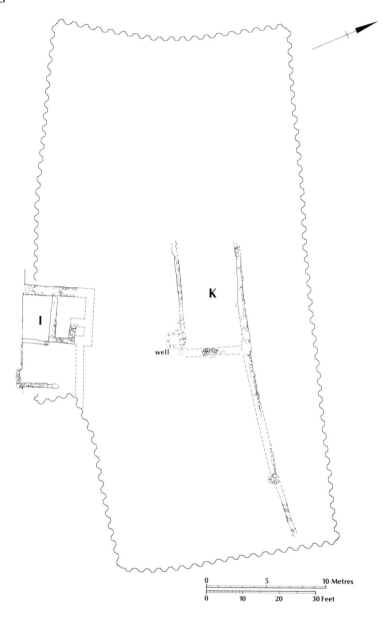

171 The Coppergate site—features surviving from the
fifteenth/sixteenth centuries, excavated before the
insertion of the perimeter shoring. Nothing from this
period remained in the western half of the site.

172 Medieval building (**I** on 171) in its final form, with cobble floor in foreground partly removed. Scale measures 1m.

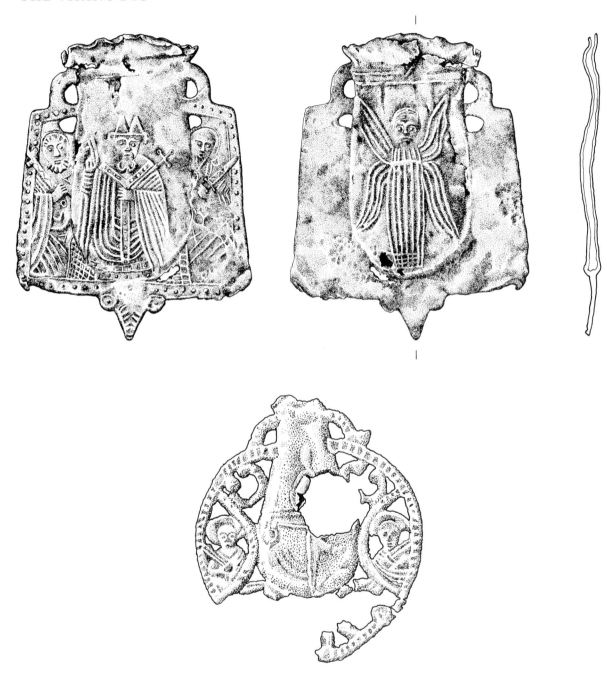

174 Lead-alloy *ampullae*. Height (*a*) 6.1cm (*b*) 7cm.

notable especially for a channel made of tiles, set on edge, which ran immediately outside the building, presumably to take away rain water (**173**, p. 128).

It is disappointing that although a wide range of building types has been excavated, the archaeological evidence does not indicate what they were used for. But there is hope that future historical work will shed some light on this problem. Many of the properties in Coppergate were owned by the Merchant Adventurers, an institution founded in 1357, whose functions included the regulation of the city's trade, as well as charitable undertakings (which are maintained to the present day). In time they acquired property rights, and it is possible that medieval documents still in their possession will provide information on who lived on the excavated tenements, and what the various buildings on them were used for. Even these properties may well have been sub-divided and sub-let, however, since this was a frequent practice in the medieval period, and reconstructing the ownership and use patterns in Coppergate from the surviving documents will be a difficult task.

Two objects found in levels broadly dated to the fourteenth century are reminders of the widespread influence of the Church at this time. Each is an *ampulla*, a small container made of lead alloy which originally held sanctified liquid obtained, at a price, at some holy site or shrine. Although their shape and decoration vary, both bear on one side representations of the same three principal figures (174 *a* and *b*). In the centre of each group is an archbishop, identifiable partly through the form of his headgear, the mitre, but principally because in one hand he is carrying a crozier, the most obvious symbol of an archbishop's insignia of office, and because he wears an archbishop's pall, the Y-shaped strips of vestment which meet at the chest. His free hand is raised in blessing. The archbishop is flanked by two figures who, as their haloes indicate, are saints. They too can be identified by the emblems which they carry—St Peter by a key, demonstrating his role as the heavenly gatekeeper, and St Paul by a sword, a reminder of his martyrdom by beheading. The appearance of these two saints signifies that the archbishop and the *ampullae* themselves have a connection with York Minster, for although the Minster is dedicated to St Peter alone, the twin saints Peter and Paul have been linked with it since the eighth century; they appear together, for example, on the principal roof boss in the Minster's fifteenth-century central tower. It therefore seems likely that these *ampullae* are religious souvenirs of the cult of Archbishop William of York, who was declared a saint in 1227.

William had a chequered career. A great-grandson of William the Conqueror, he was elected Archbishop of York in 1141, but had his appointment quashed by the Pope in 1148. Following the death of his successor as archbishop in 1153, William travelled to Rome to plead for reinstatement with a new Pope. His re-appointment confirmed, he returned to York and, according to later legend, entered the city across Ouse Bridge which collapsed after he passed, throwing many of the crowd standing upon it into the river. William's prayers ensured that everyone was rescued and this was taken as a sign of his holiness. Three weeks later William was taken ill while celebrating Mass and died shortly afterwards—the victim, it was rumoured, of poison administered in the chalice at the Mass. Within a short time it was claimed that miracles occurred at his tomb, and the Minster authorities promoted the cause of his canonisation, no doubt with one eye on rivalling the cult of Thomas Becket at Canterbury, and the other on the likely financial benefits of administering a popular shrine. Neither hope was entirely fulfilled, and St William did not achieve the national prominence of Becket or the shrine of Our Lady at Walsingham. Today, apart from fragments of the saint's tomb and shrine, both of which were broken at the Reformation, these two *ampullae* are all that survive of the cult of St William of York.

During the excavation there was no sign of the medieval waterfront on to the King's Fishpool, the large artificial lake created by damming the River Foss at York Castle. Later, during the watching brief conducted after the excavation came to an end, a group of timbers was recorded and salvaged during

175 Late medieval building (**K** on 171), cut by later features. Scale measures 1m.

the mechanical removal of soil nearer the river's present course, some 80m beyond the limits of the excavation, and they may have formed part of a revetment defining the water's edge. The timbers in the revetment were, as so often, second-hand—originally they had formed part of a ship's side. They overlapped horizontally, as medieval ships' strakes did, and they were held together by clench nails, a technique customarily used by ship-builders. The small gaps between the individual strakes had been plugged with a caulking of moss. Ships' timbers of the medieval period have only been found once before in York, and it is easily forgotten that York was an important port from its foundation until gradually eclipsed in the late Middle Ages by the growth of Hull.

The revetment is an important element in any reconstruction of how the site appeared in the medieval period but unfortunately it is not known whether the Coppergate tenement boundaries ex-tended to the waterfront, dividing it into short, separate lengths, or whether there was free access along the river's edge. However, with the Castle Mills dam intervening between the Foss and the River Ouse, it seems improbable that there was commercial development along its banks.

The overall picture of the thirteenth and four-teenth centuries at Coppergate shows the site more densely occupied than ever before in its history. The four tenements which originated c. 910 were still clearly defined, separated by roughly paved alley-ways, but now there were buildings on virtually every available space. Rubbish pits, cess pits and wells had to be crammed in wherever possible. On the street frontage the buildings were probably two or three storeys high, and even those behind them

176 View down the sixteenth-century stone-lined well shaft. Scale measures 50cm.

are likely to have been two-storeyed at least. Although repairs and replacement were still necessary from time to time, the provision of stronger foundations and the use of tiles on the roofs both slowed down the processes of rot, and helped to ensure that the buildings had a longer useful life than their predecessors. While all of these buildings might have been residential accommodation, it is equally likely that some if not all of them were also used in part for craft, industry or business, but the lack of easily recognisable groups of diagnostic objects means that at present this is uncertain. Nonetheless, the development of the Coppergate site clearly mirrors York's important commercial, administrative and social status at this time.

In the fifteenth and sixteenth centuries there was probably occupation behind the street frontage on at least three of the four tenements, but these deposits have naturally suffered more from modern disturbance than the earlier remains, and consequently the archaeological story is more patchy. On the south-central tenement, for example, an extensive reinforced cellar base had destroyed everything later than the thirteenth- to fourteenth-century pad-stone building (157 **H**). To the south the reconstructed building with stone walls and cobbled area may still have been standing and in use at this time (171 **I**), and on the northern tenement the area behind the frontage seems to have remained largely an open yard, as it had already been for about five hundred years. This leaves only the north-central tenement and, on this, badly disfigured by modern pipe trenches, there survived the walls of a structure (171 **K**), a renovated form of the pile-cluster building 157 F, which in its rebuilt form was probably occupied into the fifteenth century (175). Dwarf walls of smallish limestone rubble incorporating occasional roof tiles as levelling pieces were preserved, but they almost certainly supported a half-timbered superstructure. For once in these medieval buildings an internal feature could be recognised, a hearth or oven, but whether it was for industrial or merely domestic use is not known.

At a slightly later date, probably in the early/mid sixteenth century, a carefully constructed stone-lined well shaft, eight metres or more deep, was built just outside the new building (176). Previously it had been a succession of wood-lined, usually barrel-lined, shafts which provided a supply of water, but the new well was on a much larger and more substantial scale. Its stone lining was carefully finished to a high quality surface, and when finally removed from the shaft as surrounding layers were excavated away, some of the individual stones were found to have simple decorative mouldings of various sorts carved on one of their hidden faces, while a few even retained traces of paint. Clearly they were not initially intended for the well-shaft, but had been re-used as suitable lining material after removal from their original setting. But where did they come from? Both the nature of their decoration and the probable date of the new well combine to suggest that they were originally incorporated into one of the city's parish churches which was closed and demolished by order of the corporation in the mid sixteenth century. This had come about because a decline in York's population meant that there were too many parish churches for the number of people in the city, and there were therefore problems in maintaining some of the churches. The corporation's solution to this problem was an amalgamation of parishes and the closing of redundant churches. The church buildings were then sold off for their scrap value, and several of the city's aldermen succeeded in picking up remarkable bargains, with complete churches passing into their possession for as little as £1. Among these churches was St Peter the Little, which stood off Ousegate, only one hundred metres from the excavation site, and it is possible that this convenient source supplied the raw materials for the new well.

Near the well's base, the lowest course of stones rested on horizontal timber beams. These had slots and peg-holes cut into them which, as with the stones, clearly indicated that this was not their original resting place, and that they too had formerly been part of a building, quite possibly sections of a roof. The timbers in turn sat upon a layer of cobblestones packed in silty-clay which was immediately above the shaft's brick base (177). The

cobbles and their surrounding clay acted as a filter-bed for ground-water seeping into the shaft, and once all the back-filled debris had been removed, the well started to function again as it had done nearly four centuries before.

As the well-shaft was dismantled, the larger cutting into which it had been placed was gradually revealed. This deep hole had been potentially very dangerous when originally dug, and to counter the likelihood of collapse it had been shored up in a rough and ready way with whatever timber was available, including parts of an old door (178).

177 Re-used timber at the base of the sixteenth-century well, resting on the cobble and clay which acted as a filter bed. Scale measures 10cm.

In its construction and materials, then, this well has an interesting story to tell. It is harder to coax a very clear story from the other medieval structural remains thanks to their more fragmentary condition, but even so, they are likely to be of great interest, and after a more detailed study of all their aspects, including the associated objects, pottery

and environmental evidence, and drawing on whatever documentary evidence can be found, they may yet provide many new insights into the lives of some of York's medieval citizens. By harnessing all lines of investigation it should prove possible to be more positive not only about Coppergate's appearance in the medieval period, but also about what part it played in the city's social and economic life.

The well was the latest surviving archaeological feature excavated at Coppergate—everything relating to the seventeenth, eighteenth and early

178 Construction pit for the sixteenth-century stone-lined well, with the original shoring including a discarded wooden door. Scale measures 50cm.

nineteenth centuries had been destroyed in later rebuilding. The seventeenth- to nineteenth-century development of the site can, however, be traced on a series of plans of York, which show the four tenements at different dates in these centuries (145). Throughout the seventeenth, eighteenth and into the early years of the nineteenth century it appears that along most of Coppergate only the street frontage was built up—behind the frontages were backyards, and between them and the River Foss were gardens.

The more recent history of the site concerns the two Victorian properties which were demolished to make way for the redevelopment. They represented two amalgamations within the original four tenements, but their layout and the boundary line between them still reflected the ancient property divisions. One of these buildings was the White Horse public house, and the other was the factory of M. A. Craven & Son Ltd, manufacturers of sugar confectionery. Craven's, one of York's oldest companies, occupied the site from 1823 until 1966. They took their name from May Ann Hicks, daughter of a York confectioner, who married Thomas Craven, another York confectioner. On her father's death in 1857 the businesses were united, but her husband died in 1862, leaving her a thirty-three-year-old widow with a young son. Undaunted, she took up the management of both businesses and ran them until her death in 1900. By 1908 the workforce had quadrupled in number from two hundred to eight hundred, with Coppergate being the main production site where iced cakes and real wine jellies were made as well as sweets. After the First World War the Coppergate factory was re-named the French Almond Works, for Original Sugared Almonds had become a new line following the importation of a secret French recipe in 1900. Increased sales at home and the growth of export trade in the 1950s and 1960s, particularly to North America, Europe, Australia and Japan, led to the company vacating the Coppergate works in 1966 and moving to a new, larger site on the city's outskirts. Thus the way was clear for redevelopment and what came to be known as 'the Viking Dig'.

The new development, opened in 1984, has inherited only its outer limits from the two millennia of occupation and activity which preceded it here. But thanks to the forward vision of the site's developers, York City Council, and the interested co-operation of the contractors, Wimpey Property Holdings Ltd and their on-site personnel from Wimpey Construction Ltd, this part of York's heritage has not been bulldozed to oblivion, but instead has provided a new picture of the city's growth and development. The wealth of information summarised in the preceding chapters is now being studied by York Archaeological Trust, and will doubtless yield up even more secrets as it is investigated; the final results of this research are being published in the series *The Archaeology of York*. The story of Coppergate is also being told in another, unique, manner on the site of the excavation itself. The exceptionally well-preserved Viking Age buildings and the remarkable variety of objects found in and around them have now been conserved and replaced within the excavated area, where they were found, inside the newly constructed Jorvik Viking Centre. The underground display re-creates the picture of Viking Age Coppergate which unfolded during the excavation. The visitor is transported back through time to tenth-century York, to see a fullscale, three-dimensional simulation of how Coppergate looked at that period, with houses and workshops standing to their estimated height, a view of the River Foss waterfront (**179**, p. 129) and the scene completed with appropriate sounds and smells. All of this is based on the excavated remains which are displayed alongside so that the visitor can judge the authenticity of the simulation. This is followed by an exhibition of some of the smaller objects found during the excavation which illustrate the various aspects of life in Anglo-Scandinavian York. Throughout the Centre special effects have been created by using sophisticated display techniques, and the experience of a visit provides a well documented 'trip through time'.

The stimulus that these discoveries have given to our general archaeological knowledge, particularly of the Viking Age, is immense, but it would be a mistake to think that we now know all there is to know about Jorvik. Although the excavation will stand as a representative sample of Coppergate and its vicinity, other questions remain unanswered. Were there similar sorts of activity and occupation across the River Ouse at the crest of Bishophill, or over the Foss in the Walmgate area? How was the city defended, how was the waterfront developed, what did the cathedral church look like, what sorts of buildings were the royal palace and the earls' residence?

All these questions can be answered by careful excavation, and at York there is the possibility of learning more about the Viking Age development of a town than anywhere else in England. The Coppergate project is only a beginning in a research programme which will go on for many generations to come.

List of Donors

Financial contributors to York Archaeological Trust 1976–1982

Aksjebelskapet Freia
Arrid Nordquist
Association of Norwegian Students Abroad
Association of Voluntary Guides of York
Aurelius Charitable Trust
Bergen Bank
Bikuben Forvalten A.F.D.
A. S. Boyle
B. P. Olie-Kampaginet
British Academy
British Railways Board
Central Bank of Iceland
Chloride Group Ltd
Claxton & Garland Ltd
Courage Charitable Trust
Den Danske Bank
Drapers Charitable Trust
East Asiatic Company
Fairways Charitable Trust
Finansbanken
Forenede Chocolade Grossist
General Accident Fire & Life Assurance
Handelsbank
HRH Prince Peter
Hustru Emma Jorck's Fund
ICI Charity Trust
ICL Discretionary Trust
Illustrated Newspapers
Isaac Jackson Charity
Yvette & Hermione Jacobson Trust
Jan Lanrasbraten
Lloyds Charities Trust
Low & Bonar Charitable Fund

Magnus Magnusson
Mercers Charitable Fund
A. Moe
Samuel Montagu & Co.
Mulberry Hall
Nidor A/S
North Yorkshire County Council
Norwegian Coppergate Appeal
Egmont H. Petersen's Fund
Dame B. Philpotts Memorial Fund
Portakabin Ltd
Privatbanken
Provinsbanken
Joseph Rank Charity
Sir James Reckitt Charity
Rowntree Mackintosh Ltd
Scandinavian Bank
Scandinavian Studies Grant
S.F. Air Treatment Ltd
Shepherd Building Group
C. Ian Skipper
B. R. Snell
John & E. Sturge Ltd
Tay Charitable Trust
Joseph Terry & Sons Ltd
Tetra Pak
Tjæreborg Group
Tuborg Foundation
Twenty-Seven Foundation
Union Bank of Finland
Wallenberg Foundation
Westminster Press Ltd
F. H. Woodward Discretionary Settlement
York City Council
Yorkshire & Humberside Tourist Board

Firms who donated goods and services to York Archaeological Trust 1976–1982

Ashworth Moulds & Co
Avon Graphics
Baird & Tatlock
Barkston Ltd
Bexford Ltd
Blundell Harling Ltd
Bootham Engineers
British Rototherm Ltd
Burmatex Ltd
Cape Boards & Panels Ltd
Comark Electronics Ltd
Conair-Churchill Ltd
Copydex Ltd
Corning Ltd
Daray Lighting
Decon Ltd
John Dossor & Partners
Eurotherm Ltd
Expamet Ltd
Expanded Metal Company
A. Gallenkamp & Co Ltd
Grundfos Pumps Ltd
Gulton Europe Ltd
Heto/Uniscience Ltd
Howarth Timber Ltd

ICI Chemicals & ICI Plastics
Key Industrial Equipment Ltd
Keyways Containers Ltd
Leeds Pumping Services
Louver-Lite Ltd
Magnet Joinery
Morgan & Grundy Ltd
Nairn Floors Ltd
Netlon Ltd
Ofrex Ltd
Perkin-Elmer Ltd
Portakabin Ltd
Pumping Services Ltd
Revertex Ltd
Rolatruc Ltd
N. M. Rothschild & Sons
Seibold Ltd
Shell Chemicals
Shepherd Building Group
Tapp & Toothill Ltd
Thermographics Measurements Ltd
Torit Ltd
Union Carbide
Wallis Business Services
Wardray Products Ltd
W. C. B. Containers Ltd
Wikstrom Masonite Ltd
York Insulation Services

Index